Successful Freelancer's Mindset

Dorota Pawlak

Reviewer: Susan Gaigher

Cover design: Yassine Arrahil

Pictures on the cover: Freepik.com

ISBN: 9798365801127

Contents

What does success mean to you?

What's the recipe for success as a freelancer?

There is none.
It's up to you to create one.

For some people it will boil down to numbers flowing into their accounts every month, for others it will be about building a legacy, for some it will mean total independence, and many will probably want to have it all.

I once met a freelance translator at a conference who scoffed at people who constantly strive for more. Expensive cars, a six-figure income, luxurious holidays—it wasn't his cup of tea. His biggest dream was to be able to do what he loves: translate games. And that's what he did. With genuine pleasure. Many industry veterans considered his rates to be peanuts and deemed his lack of online presence as utterly unacceptable. This didn't bother him at all. He was free. He was living his dream life, working for himself, translating games for the local market, paying his rent and bills on time, and travelling occasionally for holidays and conferences. This was his recipe for success as a freelancer.

Back then I didn't understand this approach. Why would you agree to less if you could easily have more? How can you accept a low rate if, with some effort, you could find clients that would pay you double or triple? How can this passive lifestyle be anyone's pinnacle of success?

Now I know it can be. It's just one idea out of nearly eight billion.

Soon after this conference, the concept of a six-figure income started popping up everywhere on the Internet. It seemed like everyone in the freelance business world was talking only about this topic. Online courses were created promising that you would open and build your highly profitable business in a couple of months. Blogs and social media were filled with "real-life" stories of freelancers who made it to the magic six-digit finish line. Total madness!

When I first saw this trend, I thought: "Wow, that would be a super successful life." But then I came back to my senses: "What the ***(insert a curse word of your choice)?! If my business makes six figures, the government will probably devour half of it. What's the big deal? Why chase this unholy grail if I can't keep it all? Shall I then raise the bar and make ten figures so that I can still have six left once my taxes are paid? Utter nonsense."

And so, having a coveted six-figure business was quickly erased from my list of goals. "If it happens for me, great, if not, I'm fine"—these were my thoughts whenever I saw freelancers sharing their journeys to multifigure businesses. In all honesty, I'd prefer to make six figures from passive income or have most of my income coming from passive sources, no matter the number.

The moral of the story? Make sure your vision of success is truly yours. Regardless of what "success" society, your family, friends, or colleagues would like you to have. Of course, your definition of success may constantly evolve. As you reach new goals, you might discover that what you previously considered fabulous is now merely a starting point for an even greater adventure. Similarly, when your family situation changes, your health takes a serious turn, or your priorities shift due to various life events, you might reconsider your idea of success as a freelancer. And there's nothing wrong with that.

My idea of success has always been a work in progress. In my final year at university, my definition of success was to become a freelancer. Period. Working for myself was the peak of my dreams. Once this goal became reality, my ego desired more, year after year. First it was all about money. More clients, better projects, higher rates. Then came the desire for recognition. I used the power of social media to promote my blog, my services, and myself. It worked. In some circles I have become "famous". Next, my definition of success was extended to include regular travelling to attend translation conferences. And so, I started a journey from a shy attendee who could barely say "Hi" to a stranger, to a quite recognisable speaker who always received great feedback from her audience. Of course, it wasn't enough. After some time, my idea of success grew by two more items: publishing a book and teaching at a university. Apparently, it was still not enough, and some potential upgrade was always lurking in the back of my mind. Luckily, one little episode stopped this endless success-boosting mission. I became a mother, and my business focus changed. Actually, there was no business focus at all. For nearly two years. But when my foggy baby brain finally disappeared and I could think more clearly again, my priorities and definition of success were reformulated once again. Now it's all about being free. Free from the race and flitting desires. Free to choose where, how, and whom I work with. Free to build a passive income so I can stay free.

On a less egoistic level, it's about making the lives of my clients, readers, and students a little bit easier.

That's my definition of success as a freelancer. What's yours?

1. Why is the right mindset important?

No matter how you define your success as a freelancer, you may realise that reaching your goal will require some sort of super power. It's like chasing unicorns on the other side of the rainbow.

Making your dream come true might seem to be a mission impossible. Luckily, there are always ways to make your journey less painful and tools to make it more realistic. The right connections, skills, resources, and strategies are all extremely important. However, there's one more important ingredient that can determine whether you fail or sail: the right approach.

I'm sure you've heard about professional athletes who—despite all the talent and hard work—fail to win gold medals, beat new records, or score that essential point. On the other hand, there are countless examples of people who made it to the top despite their lack of extraordinary talent or significant resources, like first-class equipment and coaches, because they leveraged the power of visualisation. They focused on the right mindset. Arnold Schwarzenegger, Lindsey Vonn, and Michael Phelps are just a few of many inspiring achievers who visualised their way to the top. Scientific research confirms the effectiveness of mental preparation. For example, as part of a famous study in the 1960s, Alan Richardson divided participants into three groups. Group 1 practised free throws for 30 days, group 2 visualised successful free throws for 30 days, whereas group 3 didn't practise or visualise. At the end of the experiment, the group that only practised physically improved by 24%, the group that didn't do any work showed no improvement at all, and the group that visualised their success improved by 23%.[1] It turned out that mental practise was nearly as effective as physical practise. Imagine what could happen if you combine these two together! Or think again about athletes who train and visualise their results... Since Richardson's experiment, many other studies have confirmed that mental preparation plays a key role, not only in the sports world, but in every other area of life, including business.

Your beliefs shape your thoughts, which in turn shape your behaviour. Of course, the right mindset alone won't guarantee quick success. You can't simply repeat in your head "I will achieve it" to see extra digits in your bank account. Merely thinking about your success every single day won't suffice to build a profitable business, hit another sales record, publish your book, or reach one million followers on your YouTube channel. Whatever your goal is, you need a balanced mixture of all the ingredients: experience, tools, connections, hard work, skills, and the right mindset as a strong foundation to build on.

What is that "right mindset?" It's not only about visualising your success. There's much more to it than believing you can achieve it. It's about being ready to grow, learn, and adapt.

For more than four decades, Carol Dweck has been researching mindset, motivation, and failure. In her book, *Mindset: The*

---

[1] Alan Richardson, "Mental Practice: A Review and Discussion Part I," *Research Quarterly. American Association for Health, Physical Education and Recreation* 38, no. 1 (1967): pp. 95-107, https://doi.org/10.1080/10671188.1967.10614808.

New Psychology of Success, she states that every individual has either a growth or a fixed mindset.[2] With a fixed mindset, you believe that your intelligence and abilities are innate. When you fail, you give up and blame your lack of skills. When you hear the word "success", you only see your own success, and you crave constant praise for your achievements. However, with a growth mindset, you believe that you can overcome any hurdles. You know that your intelligence, talents, or abilities can always be developed if you invest enough time and effort, and you persevere. If you fail, you analyse what happened and draw conclusions from your experience to achieve better results next time. Whenever you feel you're not good at something, you know that you're not where you want to be <u>yet.</u> With this approach, anything may seem possible. And that's the component that will build the "right mindset", the basis for your success.

Your mindset does play an important role in your success. It may slow you down or push you forward. Let's take a look at how you can transform your thoughts and beliefs to turn your freelance career into a rewarding adventure.

---

[2] Carol S. Dweck, *Mindset: The New Psychology of Success* (New York: Random House, 2006).

2. What is stopping you from living a successful freelance life?

Many freelancers claim that they are a work in progress. Some pieces perfectly fit their success puzzle, some are still missing, and some seem to be unachievable. Since I became a freelancer in 2011, I began paying more attention to how other small business owners and solopreneurs pave their way towards their goals. I once met a lawyer whose wildest dream was to open her own cafe. After working many hours in her regular office job, she would go back home to bake cakes and pastries for her clients: custom wedding cakes, birthday cakes in all shapes and colours—little pieces of joy for every possible occasion. Our paths crossed when I wanted to order my bizarre wedding cake in the form of a globe. She invited me to her home to discuss my wishes and to understand my ideas. Then she built a model of the globe from Styrofoam (3-D printing wouldn't become common for another couple of years) to make sure that the cake would have the right shape. The result was breath-taking. There was no doubt that she was a talented confectioner. When it came to paying her, my jaw dropped. What? Merely 300 euro for this masterpiece? I had expected the price to be as high as the quality of her creation. It did not matter to me that she was still in the transition phase from a busy lawyer to a future cafe owner. It did not bother me that she baked at home, had no fancy business name (yet), and no posh location. What mattered was the result and her amazing customer service with that personal touch. When I went to pick up my cake, I told her how much I admired her work and suggested that she increase her rates. She replied with a humble smile. Fast-forward five years, and her dream has come true. She now owns a small cafe where she bakes her masterpieces full time, employing others to keep her business growing, and charging the right price for her unique confectionery.

Every time I think about this story, I realise that in some societies, talking about and desiring money are deeply rooted taboos. In some cultures, being humble is one of the most desired virtues to have in your friend, colleague, or employee. It might take years to get rid of the "I'm not worth it" mentality and switch to an "aggressive business mode," which is not that aggressive at all. I was stuck there for too long. In my early years of freelancing, I was guilty of all errors typical to those brought up to value humility and to avoid conflict, failure, and the topic of money. I charged too little, cried when someone pointed out my mistakes, and was absolutely convinced that my "one-person business" didn't deserve to be called a business at all. After all, I was "just" a translator, working from a home office, not in a posh downtown location. I was "just" an expat, barely speaking the language of my new country, too shy to even try to network with other business owners to learn, grow, and overcome hurdles.

I'm sure your path hasn't been a bed of roses either.

No matter what your definition of success is, there's always something that you need to change, add, remove, or transform. There's always a distance that you need to cover to get from where you are now to where you want to be. To close that gap, you'll need the right tools, thought patterns, and action plans. Being talented, skilled, educated, experienced in marketing, accountancy, customer acquisition, or risk management may not be enough to shape the freelancing career of your dreams. Whether your goal is to become a six-figure business owner, innovator, prolific writer, or life-time digital nomad, you may stumble over similar obstacles. Fear of criticism, low self-esteem, aversion to failure, or constant procrastination may become your biggest enemies regardless of your knowledge and experience.

Let's figure out how to identify these enemies and eliminate them from your business life.

2.1 Fear of failure

Have you ever locked yourself out of your apartment? Have you ever forgotten your passport on the way to the airport or left your luggage on the train?

These little moments of clumsiness happen to everyone. Usually, they're not life-threatening, nor do they put your financial situation at risk. Yet, the way you react to such setbacks may reveal a lot about your likelihood to succeed as a business owner. That's because failure is an inseparable part of both private and business life. To be able to grow, you need to learn how to deal with failure, how to get ready for potential pitfalls, and how to draw conclusions from any misfortune. In this section, you'll find some helpful strategies for approaching your failures in a graceful way. But first, let's step back and focus on the paralysis that prevents you from acting even before you fail (or succeed).

Some people don't leave their houses because they are afraid of failing. Some people don't travel because of their fear of getting sick, losing their belongings, missing the flight, or being disappointed. The same anxiety may overpower you on your freelancing path, especially if you want to move from full-time employment to solopreneurship. What if I don't find enough customers to sustain my business? What if my business never offers me more than my current comfortable salary and all the nice perks? What if no one buys my new products? What if no one chooses my services no matter how much effort I put into marketing, networking, and promoting?

The "what if…" mantra can easily become a persistent earworm. It will paralyse you, suffocate you, wrap you tightly, take away your voice, energy, and vision. It will quickly turn your worst-case scenario into a reality. It will become your nightmare. Fear of failure is one of the deadliest dream stealers, both in business and personal life. You might have a great idea, but you're scared to act upon it. You might be given a perfect opportunity to finally open your handicraft shop, yoga studio, or dental practice, but you dread taking a loan to renovate your potential business location, and you're afraid to invest your savings in the necessary equipment. After days of pondering, you let the opportunity pass, just to see someone else taking over your dream space and filling it with your idea. A new handicraft shop, yoga studio, or dental practice comes to life right in front of you, but it's not you who will be called the mother/father of its success. Maybe at that point you try to console yourself by saying that the new business owner probably had rich parents, a wealthy partner, or made an incredible amount of money from some other business venture. As magical as it may seem, such scenarios are rarely true. In most cases, the difference between that successful businessperson next door and you—still stuck in the dream phase—is fear. Fear of failing and taking risks. How can you overcome this fear?

Befriend your enemy
Do what psychologists do when they treat phobias and anxiety disorders: apply exposure therapy.

Imagine you were afraid of heights. Applying exposure therapy would entail gradually exposing yourself to heights under controlled conditions. You'd visualise yourself climbing a high mountain or taking an elevator to the 10th, 20th or 30th floor until you become comfortable with these levels. You'd use relaxation techniques, such as deep breathing and mindfulness, to stay calm. These small steps would help your brain deal with the feared stimulus. By repeating your exposure, you'd finally realise that the danger isn't real. After some time, you'd feel ready to face your fear in real life. And you'd do so with no heart palpitations, no paralysis, and no drama.

You can apply the same method to fight your business fears. Your exposure plan could be as follows:

Imagine your worst-case scenario
Ask yourself: what's the worst thing that could happen? How will your life change if your loyal customers turn you down, if your investment fails, or if your business partner runs away with your money? How would you react? What would be your quick recovery plan?

Many freelancers are reluctant to increase their rates, especially for their regular customers. What if the new price scares my clients? What if they replace me with someone cheaper? These are the kind of thoughts that might stop you from adjusting your prices. First of all, if your customers are only focused on the "cheap" side of the project triangle, maybe they're not the right match for you. In most cases your customers keep coming back to you because they value the quality of your services/products and the relationship they have with you. A slight price increase, especially in times of heavy inflation (like when I'm writing these words in 2022), should be acceptable to most clients. Either way, prepare your action plan for the worst-case scenario, or—even better—be proactive by attracting new customers that are ready to pay your increased price. Then, the fear of losing your regular customers after your price adjustment should decrease, giving you more courage to act.

Usually, the worst-case scenario isn't as bad as it seemed once you've analysed it thoroughly and developed quick-recovery procedures. In fact, very often it doesn't happen at all. By being prepared for the worst, you can reduce your fear and come up with a strategy to prevent any potential disasters.

Take baby steps

Break down your overwhelming business idea into small bits. For example, if you're convinced that you'll lose your customers once you raise your rates, you can start by informing only one or two clients about your price increase. You probably have some customers who pay you less than your current standard rate or clients who send you projects that you're not entirely happy to work on. Begin your rate-adjustment journey with these accounts. Also, make sure you don't scare your clients with the planned rate increase: 10% to 15% should be enough for a start and acceptable to most clients. See how your process goes, adapt your strategy if needed, then proceed with the next step. Maybe your clients will respond positively, and maybe they won't even notice that your rate is higher. That would be a good sign to contact your remaining customers as well and inform them about your rate change.

Fear of failure might also appear when you need to speak in front of a large audience. In this case, your first baby step would be to start attending business events in your region. You wouldn't even have to talk to anyone, but rather watch, listen, and analyse. After a while, you might feel ready for small talk with random attendees, or maybe you'd even be brave enough to ask questions during the Q&A session at a conference. The next step would be to deliver a brief presentation in front of a small group. Then increase the size of your audience, location, and presentation until your comfort zone expands and you feel at ease speaking in front of a large group. With regular exposure, your fear will begin to diminish. You'll also pick up new skills and develop mastery that will help reduce the need to worry at all.

If your main business fear is the transition from full-time employment to freelancing, you can take baby steps to make this transformation as smooth as possible. For example, you can work on your business part time while also working for your employer, until you see that your side hustle has potential to become your main business. You can also choose to continue working full time and work on your business on the weekends and evenings until your project becomes profitable enough for you to relinquish your fear and quit your job. Yet another scenario is to build a buffer before you quit your full-time employment and move to freelancing. You can save money to cover five to six months of your expenses, then leave your employer and start working on your business only. In this way, your fear of failure should gradually decrease, giving you resources and confidence to be truly free. Of course, overcoming your fear of failure in your business might not be enough to guarantee instant success. You still need other essential ingredients, such as a clear action plan, specific strategies on how to attract and retain your clients, how to close sales, and how to present your products or your offer in an appealing way.

Focus on the fun side

Focus on what? Is there any fun in fear of failure? Believe it or not, every situation and every challenge has an enjoyable side. Even if you're scared to take the first step, there must be something you'll enjoy about the process. For example, you might feel overwhelmed to go to a networking event, but you know that the event will be held in an amazing place and that delicious food will be served for all attendees. You can shift your focus from what scares you (failing to make valuable contacts) to what can lift you up (absorbing new sounds, shapes, colours, or tastes). In this way, you'll push the unpleasant aspects of your challenge into the background, which will help you stay calm and relaxed. What's the biggest benefit of this approach? You'll probably achieve more than you would if you only focused on the overwhelming task (such as meeting new people, talking about your business, etc.). And even if you don't "achieve" anything and leave the event with no new clients, business partners, or ideas, you'll at least realise that you can enjoy your time even when the circumstances paralyse you and your fear of failure seems to take your breath away.

The art of graceful failure

Sometimes it's not fear of failure that limits your actions, but your inability to deal with the failure itself. This in turn can instil or reignite your fear of failing. So, how can you learn to fail gracefully? How can you make sure that you learn from your business failures, change your strategies, and eventually grow? How can you approach any mishap with a growth mindset?

Be prepared

In business, like in life, things rarely go smoothly. That's why it's wise to be ready for potential rejections, failures, and mistakes. Naturally, you don't need to draw up a meticulous risk-management plan (although this may come in handy!), but at least try to be mentally prepared. Even if you consider yourself extremely lucky, smart, resilient, business-oriented, professional, and cautious, it would be dangerous to assume that the good things will last forever. Everything in life is temporary. It might be one year, two, or 20, but eventually your road will become bumpy. A constant belief in good luck may shatter your stable position when tough times come. To stay on the safe side, relish the good times, but stay alert and ready to accept any turn of fate.

Analyse and act

Whether you've lost a loyal customer or invested a large sum in a marketing campaign that didn't work—make sure to step back and analyse what went wrong. Ask yourself why it happened. What can you do better next time to avoid similar situations? Maybe you can delegate your marketing to a more experienced team or improve your customer service? Maybe you had too much on your plate and failed to control every single process in your business? By evaluating your situation and drawing valid conclusions, you'll be able to identify your weak spots, implement new strategies, and act more efficiently next time. It also helps to ask for feedback to find out how your failure looked from the perspective of your clients, business partners, colleagues, or family.

For example, I once lost a very reputable potential client, only because I delayed replying to their e-mail. In the last step of the vendor-selection process, I was asked to present my portfolio to prove that I had worked on similar projects. Of course, I was able to deliver such proof, but this request simply overwhelmed me at the time, so I kept procrastinating. As a mother of a six-month-old baby, I was probably too distracted (all hail the baby brain…) to smoothly turn on my super professional business mode after a sleepless night and long hours of breastfeeding. Of course, the company chose someone else, which taught me a valuable lesson. Now, every request for a quote that comes from a potentially perfect client receives my due care.

Practice non-attachment

Sometimes failures, no matter how painful or costly, are not necessarily your fault. There are hundreds of external factors outside of your control. One such factor was the coronavirus pandemic that forced thousands of freelancers and small business owners to close, suspend, or reinvent their activities. When your business fails, it doesn't mean that you're a failure too.

To be ready to act wisely, learn, tweak, improve, and grow, you need to detach yourself from your business and your failure. This might be hard, especially for freelancers. After all, in your solo business nearly all decisions are made by you, so who else should take responsibility for a failure? It may sound like a schizophrenic move, but sometimes it helps to realise that you as a business owner are not the same person as you in your personal life. This perspective will provide you with some healthy distance to assess and cope with any rejection, failure, or mistake. You'll find out more about practising non-attachment in Chapter 4.2.

Move on

No matter what happens, don't let the failure stop you. Think about other motivating business owners, writers, athletes, or artists who didn't give up even when life gave them lemons. J. K. Rowling's book was rejected 12 times before it became an overnight success. Harland Sanders was rejected 1009 times before his recipe was finally accepted and Kentucky Fried Chicken was born. It took Melanie Perkins three years to find investors for her start-up and lead Canva to global success.

Take their stories as a powerful inspiration and turn any "no" into "not yet". Maybe the world is not ready for your success yet, maybe you are not ready to reach your goal right now. When a failure or rejection hits you hard, turn the experience into an opportunity to work harder and smarter. Tweak your plans, find new ways to implement your ideas, and embrace setbacks as inevitable (but illuminating!) parts of your business adventure.

Frontline stories: how I befriended my fear of failure

As a young freelancer, I was convinced that public speaking is an essential step to position myself as an expert in the industry. There was only one problem: I was extremely shy and afraid of failure. Focused on my "why", I hesitantly submitted my first conference proposal. To my surprise, it was accepted. I had to prepare myself for this paralysing adventure. Using the gradual-exposure technique, I managed to overcome my shyness and combat my fear of failure, criticism, and judgement. I spent three months reading, researching, and writing my speech. As if that wasn't enough, I also enrolled in two courses on public speaking. Then I asked my friend, a professional voice coach, for her valuable advice. To be on the safe side, I wrote down every single word of my future speech. I kept memorising it and increasing my test audience until I felt ready to speak in front of a large group of translators who came to my presentation on creativity in software localisation at the second IAPTI Conference in Athens in 2014. Luckily, all this hard work paid off. My speech received quite positive feedback, which helped me realise that my fear had been bigger than the reality. Although I don't present regularly anymore, I usually need only two to three weeks to prepare my speech, and I definitely don't spend as much time on rehearsals as I did eight years ago. A little fear might still be lurking in the corner of my mind, but instead of being as huge and blinding as the sun, it has now decreased to the size of a sunflower seed.

Fear of failure may be overwhelming, but only if you feed its growth. With the right strategy, you'll be able to eradicate it. Focus on the method that works best for you, such as taking small steps, drafting a plan B, overpreparing yourself for the event that scares you, or analysing the worst-case scenario.

No matter what strategy you choose to overcome your fear, one thing is definite: Fighting your fear of failure means exposing yourself to that fear step by step. So, maybe failing a few times won't be such a terrible experience, especially if it helps you to draw conclusions, adjust your work style, and realise that, with the right preparation, you can survive or even thrive from any failure.

2.2 Fear of criticism

Another beast that can easily feed off your energy and diminish your courage to act is fear of criticism. How can you recognise this fear and make sure it stays away from your freelance business?

When my first book *You've got this: How to continue your freelance career when you become a mother* was published, one of the readers contacted me to share her story. She thanked me for the motivation to start working on her business but also painted a picture of her limitations. She was tired of her mother/housewife responsibilities and had come up with a wonderful idea for a business. But she was scared. "What will my family say if I tell them that from now on our child has to spend more time at the nursery so I can work? How do I explain to my husband, my parents, and his parents that I won't necessarily become a worse mother when I open my business?" These were the questions that were dominating her thoughts and consuming her energy that could have been better spent drafting a strategy for her future business. The fear of being judged as an irresponsible, selfish, or greedy mother prevented her from creating a job she would love. She didn't think that she might fail to attract customers or generate a good profit. Her only limiting thought was: "What will people say?"

Are similar thoughts hurting you as well? Are you trying to connect with people, but you're not sure how they will react when you tell them about your business? Do you want to engage with people on social media, but before posting anything you double-check the content and analyse how your followers will react? Are you more concerned about being labelled as aggressive, self-centred, or arrogant when promoting your services? Or maybe you would love to present your ideas at an industry event, but you're worried about being criticised?

Most of my freelance colleagues have felt this type of paralysis at least once in their career. I've been there many times as well. Even now, writing these words, I'm worried about being judged. But you know what? I slash this fear with my "why", and that spooky monster instantly crumbles and hides away (hopefully not under my daughter's bed).

How can I deal with the fear of criticism?
The first step is to realise that your fear of being criticised usually appears when you let others define you. This in turn happens when you're not truly convinced of who you are, and—as Luvvie Ajayi Jones puts it—"whose you are."[3] In other words, it's not enough to know what
your core values, beliefs, and ambitions are. You also have to know what your role is in
society. Where do you belong? Would you be able to answer the question "Who are you?" without mentioning obvious adjectives, such as your nationality or profession? Your answer doesn't have to be unique, deep, or thought-provoking, but it has to truly paint a picture of you as an individual human and you as a member of a group. Not just any group, but one where you feel comfortable, where you have the courage to be yourself. This might be your family, local church, sport's club, book club, discussion club, association, volunteer organisation,

---

[3] Ajayi Luvvie Jones, *Professional Troublemaker: The Fear Fighter Manual* (New York: Viking, 2021).

or any other social entity where you're happy to contribute, co-exist, and co-create without any fear. This is the "whose you are" factor that will help you create your own definition of yourself.

Once you have a clear image of yourself, the thoughts and words of other people should have less of an impact on your actions. But even then, your self-awareness and self-confidence might fail to protect you from the creeping fear of judgement. Especially in the business environment, where everything may seem more serious and overwhelming. Then your action plan could be as follows:

Focus on your why
When you do something in a different way, introduce new services or innovative products, most people will not understand you. When you want to leave your stable full-time employment to embark on an unpredictable freelancing path, your family and friends may start judging you. But your main shield is your "Why". As Simon Sinek puts it in his excellent books,[4] you need to know why you do what you do. What inspires you to work? Why did you open your business? Why do you get out of bed every morning? Don't stop at the most obvious answers such as "I need to make a decent living." Keep the dialogue with yourself going by asking more detailed questions. Why do you feel you need make a decent living? Why by running a business? Why this business? In this industry? With these people? You can search for your "Why"

---

[4] Simon Sinek. *Start with Why: How Great Leaders Inspire Everyone to Take Action* (New York: Penguin, 2011.); Simon Sinek. *Find Your Why: A Practical Guide for Discovering Purpose for You and Your Team* (New York: Penguin, 2017.)

within your values, passions, strengths, and motivations, or you can conduct a short self-experiment. For example, you can describe your ideal workday, then analyse it for clues about your "Why". You can also think about activities that give you a true sense of fulfilment and ask yourself why you feel this way.

You do what you do not only to earn money (hopefully). There's something else that motivates you to get up every morning, meet with your customers, and help them make their lives easier. Maybe your "Why" is to help people communicate better, maybe it's to show them how to lead a happy and healthy life, or maybe to support them in expressing their creative ideas. No matter what the nature of your freelance business, shift the focus from your "What" and "How" to your "Why". With this approach, you'll not only be able to overcome your fears, but you'll also find clarity in your life, stay focused on your goals, and make the right decisions.

It's not about you
Several studies have shown[5] that our fear of being negatively judged are usually overestimated. We anticipate a harsh reaction after a mishap or social blunder, but the reaction of other individuals is not usually as negative as we had expected. Our fear of being criticised is exaggerated because we tend to focus too much on our misfortunes and failures. Thus, instead of thinking intensively about the possible outcomes of our

---

[5] Kenneth Savitsky, Nicholas Epley, and Thomas Gilovich, "Do Others Judge Us as Harshly as We Think? Overestimating the Impact of Our Failures, Shortcomings, and Mishaps.," *Journal of Personality and Social Psychology* 81, no. 1 (2001): pp. 44-56, https://doi.org/10.1037/0022-3514.81.1.44.

actions, a better approach might be to simply do our job as well as we can without pondering how it will be assessed. In most cases it won't be evaluated at all, because most people are too busy minding their own business. For each of us, the world revolves around ourselves. Everyone is so concerned with their own needs, goals, and problems that no one will probably give your speech, website, social media post, or business idea a second thought once they leave the event or shift their focus to a more important task. Even if harsh judgement hits you, it helps to remember that the painful words might only represent what the other person thinks about her/his own situation. For example, if someone says: "Oh look at her with all those fancy clothes teaching us how to run a profitable business," they probably mean "Oh, I wish I could look so elegant and successful." If someone tells you: "You're so salesy with your tweets, can't you simply share something valuable?", it might mean that they wish they had the courage to promote their own services as well.

Of course, sometimes the negative feedback you receive is valid, but again, it's not really about you. It's about your work, your behaviour. The fact that someone pointed out mistakes on your website doesn't mean that you're a terrible designer. It only means that your website needs some tweaks to become flawless. Don't take feedback too personally, and focus on the actual message.

Find a grain of truth
It might be difficult to admit, but sometimes the criticism you hear might be well-founded. To determine whether you should treat harsh words seriously, first consider the form and the source. Does the feedback come from a person you trust? Are

they experts in the field in question? Is their feedback constructive or is it nothing more than hate speech? Sieve through the words to detect the real meaning.

Take art critics, for example. They tend to give brutally honest opinions, believing that authors seek feedback. They strive to challenge the content they're viewing to help create better art.[6] That's also the approach of many brilliant teachers who push their students to their limits. Although the methods they use or words they say may be harsh and unorthodox, their main goal is to help their students fulfil their true potential. I'm sure you've come across such teachers on your path as well. In case you haven't, think about (or watch) the movie *Whiplash*. It's a perfect example of strict but effective teaching where constructive criticism eventually makes the student's talent shine. Of course, many people (including myself) are too sensitive to negative evaluation and would rather hear some encouraging comments before they're ready to hear about their weaknesses. But the person who is criticising you might not know you well enough to realise that. They want to help, show you how to become perfect, hence the criticism. Even if you're convinced that the negative feedback about your behaviour isn't valid, it's worth taking some time to analyse it. Maybe your actions could be improved, maybe you're not as successful with closing sales as you had thought, maybe your business communication could be improved. If you're unsure, always ask for a second opinion, talk to experts, see how other business owners approach the specific task, and then identify your areas for improvement.

---

[6] Albert Williams, "What Makes a Critic Tick?," Chicago Reader, July 4, 2002, https://chicagoreader.com/news-politics/what-makes-a-critic-tick/.

Sometimes people criticise others in good faith, they just fail to put their comments in an elegant form. Sometimes they don't want to be mean, they just want to wake you up, help you avoid mistakes, and let that unpolished diamond shine. Perhaps changing your approach to criticism will let you turn any negative feedback into a useful tool; one that shows you how to become a better person and a more successful business owner.

Stop criticising others

Maybe the reason you think other people judge you is because you keep criticising others? You judge the world around you—aloud or in your head—and you're convinced that your actions are constantly scrutinised as well. Sometimes we treat other people as our "mirror". We may assign them our thoughts, values, and expectations. For example, you might consider your colleagues to be jealous of your success because that's what you would feel if someone you know had built a profitable business in your industry. You might think that the group of strangers you meet at a networking event is arrogant and unaware of any newcomers because that's how you would act if you came to an event with a group of your colleagues. You're convinced that a person you barely know would welcome your unsolicited opinion because that's how your mentors or parents behaved. We often assume that other people are an extension of our "tribe", subconsciously projecting both our negative and positive features onto them. The same happens with judgement. Your fear of being criticised might be related to the little judge inside you. The first step to get rid of that beast is to observe your thoughts.

Whenever you notice your inner judge condemning a person for an aggressive tweet, salesy presentation, poor communication skills, or any other action that in your view isn't "compliant" with business behaviour, simply picture a large stop sign in your mind. That's how you can remind yourself to shift your thoughts into another, more positive direction. The next step is to understand that person. Maybe she/he has a valid reason to act the way they act. Maybe he's new to the industry and simply uses marketing techniques acceptable in other fields. Maybe she has just opened her business and needs more experience to act in a more confident way. Maybe the person you labelled as aggressive is simply following the guidelines of their marketing mentor. Try to imagine their background, or even better, talk to them to learn about their backstory. The next step is to accept others for what they are. It might be difficult to let go of your need to change others, but that's an essential step if you want to avoid frustration and disappointment when communicating and collaborating with them.

Sometimes you will meet people on your freelance business path who should be made aware of their inappropriate actions. However, as long as their behaviour isn't illegal and doesn't put anyone's health or safety at risk, you may want to share your feedback in a constructive and friendly manner. Don't judge that person, but rather indicate areas for improvement. Highlight the good points and suggest how they can tweak their presentations, social media posts, marketing campaigns, or customer service.

The key to success is to move the focus from criticising what other business owners do to your own actions. Convert that judgemental energy into a creative power that will help you find understanding and inspiration even in the most awkward situations.

Don't criticise yourself

The little critic that lives inside of you might be focused on your actions only. It might be the reason for your fear of criticism. Maybe you keep creating stories about how you're supposed to behave, how your business should grow, or how much profit you should make. Maybe you set the bar too high for yourself, trying to be perfect in every single field. We'll talk about perfectionism in Chapter 2.5. For now, just make sure you lower your standards to realistic levels. You can't ace every task. You can't be an excellent marketer, successful business owner, brilliant investor, superb speaker, outstanding writer, and top-notch designer all in one person. Everyone has strong and weak points, and you'll probably excel in only a few areas, be mediocre at some, and perform poorly at many. But that's perfectly fine. Instead of beating yourself up for not meeting your own high standards, you can collaborate with someone else who could compensate for all your weak points. However, if you desperately want to do as many things as possible in your business, don't blame yourself for not being perfect. Rather enrol in a course, consult with an expert, or read several books to increase your knowledge and level of confidence.

To silence your inner critic, you can use a similar method to the one described above. Whenever you notice that you're judging yourself, stop your thoughts and shift your focus to something else. Notice what was positive in your behaviour; what went well with your presentation, negotiations, or e-mail communication. If you did make a mistake, apologise, repair,

Frontline stories: how I befriended my fear of criticism
There was a time in my career when I was deeply concerned about how other people perceived my business. Shortly after embarking on my freelance adventure, I became obsessed that I might be negatively judged for being "only" a translator. To mitigate this uncomfortable feeling, I kept coming up with new business names, trying to implement corporate-like branding and reinvent my marketing strategy. All that for the fear of not being treated seriously, being laughed at for my silly services, business names, logos, or websites. I got so caught up with what my potential clients or colleagues might say about my business name, logo, or branding that I completely forgot to focus on why I do what I do. Instead of concentrating on my strengths, I became fixated on my unreal limitations. "My business is too small for big brands, I'm too expensive compared to translators based in Poland, my Dutch is not good enough to collaborate with Dutch companies…" The reasons my potential customers wouldn't work with me were flowing into my head like a herd of wild horses. Of course, there were many business opportunities for me in the Dutch and the international market, but I was too concerned about being criticised to be able to take advantage of them. Luckily, I found a way out of these limiting thoughts by reigniting my passion. After long hours of talking with experts from various fields, reading tons of business books, and building up my self-confidence, I stopped worrying about how other people perceived my work. A few years ago, my fear of criticism nearly evaporated: My priorities shifted when I became a mother. Since work wasn't the top priority anymore, many of my fears, and dilemmas around my business lost their destructive power.

2.3 Fear of rejection

Our journey through our limiting fears finally leads to the core of the matter. Fear of rejection is the underlying cause of fear of criticism, and it's strongly related to our fear of failure. For some people, failing means being rejected, and criticism is just another word for being a misfit, excluded from the group they aspire to be a part of. Since humans are a social species, most of us want to belong and feel connected to others. Thousands of years ago people had to be a part of the tribe to survive. Being excluded from the group was equivalent to dying alone in the wild. Although nowadays you probably won't die after being rejected, exclusion is still an extremely painful experience. It might be interpreted as "you're not one of us," "you're not worth connecting with us," "you're not enough." That's why fear of rejection is so powerful. It can easily prevent you from pursuing your goals and adhering to your values.

How can fear of rejection manifest in your business life?

Imagine your colleague asks you for help with an urgent task. You're already busy with other projects, but she helped you last time when you were overwhelmed with work, so you feel you need to "pay her back." You don't want to jeopardise your good relationship, thus you reluctantly say yes, even though helping her would mean staying up the whole night or giving up your social plans to complete the urgent request.

As another example, imagine a client requests a quick online meeting to briefly discuss your next project. You want to prove you're a valuable partner and show that you're open to long-term collaboration, so you put all your current tasks on hold to meet his expectations. What was supposed to be a quick call turns out to be a one-hour long discussion, and now you regret that you didn't clarify upfront how much time you can assign for this call or rejected his request in the first place.

Finally, imagine the most common situation in a freelancer's life: increasing your rates. This is a topic that never ceases to be trendy, at least in the freelance translator's world. What if I lose my clients if I raise my rates? What if they won't work with me again? These concerns stem from a fear of rejection and may haunt you regardless of your experience. I remember discussing this topic at an online conference once. Each of the attendees had been running their businesses for many years, but this fear was still lingering in all of our heads. One fellow business owner had just increased his rates before the infamous 2022 inflation, so he was hesitant to do it again. Another colleague was worried that her clients would leave her and choose a cheaper vendor (her competition) who hadn't adjusted their rates. My idea was to start increasing my prices gradually, beginning with the clients who had the least exciting projects or the lowest rates. Thus, even if they rejected my price adjustment, I wouldn't regret losing them too much. But none of us did anything. The possibility of being turned down, losing our regular clients or income, kept us passive for too long. When I finally informed my clients about my higher rates (nearly one month after the moment I discussed it with my peers), they accepted it without any questions. In fact, a day after I informed one of my clients about the slight price increase, they contacted me with a new project, of course agreeing to pay the new rate. Had I known it would be so easy,

I would have implemented my idea straight away without wasting time and energy on all the worst-case scenarios.

Fear of rejection has many faces. It's usually expressed as a difficulty to say no, refusing to ask for what you want or need, working too hard to satisfy others, accepting too many tasks, being overly sensitive to criticism, or blaming yourself when things don't work out. When these behaviours become your daily routine, your road to a successful freelance business becomes long and twisty. Let's have a look at some ideas that will help you deal with rejection and stick to your goals even when you're filled with fear.

Find the reason
There's probably nothing more confusing than getting a dry "no" as an answer. Whether you're bidding on an interesting project, sending a quote to your ideal prospect, or trying to start a beneficial collaboration—a negative reply is painful if it's not followed by any explanation. It might also be the reason you fear being rejected. Not knowing why someone doesn't want to work with you on a particular project can make you believe there's something wrong with you, while in fact there could be a myriad of reasons.

Your quote might have been turned down because it's too high, because you sent your proposal too late, or because your clients cancelled the project or decided to use a service provider recommended by their network—you'll never know why you received a negative answer if you don't ask. Asking for the reason might be terrifying, but that's the only way to receive valuable input. It will also help you realise that rejection doesn't necessarily relate to you as a person; there might simply be a mismatch between your offer and your customer's expectations. For example, you might learn that you're the ideal person to work with, but your client had to postpone the project or was looking for a cheaper vendor (this has happened to me so many times!). You might discover that the initial plan to work with a freelancer was abandoned, and now your potential client is looking for a big agency. Maybe you'll learn that your business partners would like to work with you on a new project but have too much on their plate right now, thus they have temporarily put their plans on hold.

In some cases, you won't have to ask for the reason at all. It will be right there in plain text or hidden between the lines. It's then your call to decide whether there's anything you can adapt to avoid being rejected in the future or whether you should simply move on. And that's how we arrive at step two.

Learn your lesson

If your proposal, idea, quote, or application gets rejected, it's not the end of the world. It can be a wonderful opportunity to grow. Once you know the reason behind the negative answer, break it down to draw conclusions. Turn a painful "no" into your future action plan.

For example, if you find out that your proposal arrived too late, make sure you respond to your client's messages more quickly in future. If you learn that your message accidently ended up in the client's spam folder, take steps to make sure your e-mails can get through spam filters. If your client tells you that your services are too expensive, try to highlight the benefits of working with you, or add more precise information on what your offer includes next time you send a quote. The price isn't always the main deciding factor. Once your clients understand the quality of your work, they might be ready to pay more.

On the other hand, sometimes rejection has nothing to do with your behaviour, rates, reviews, or communication style. The real reason might be beyond your control. For example, when your client suddenly has to cancel a project to limit expenses or when your business partner has to postpone collaborating with you due to personal issues. Accept such a turn of events and proceed to the next step.

Move on and succeed next time

With every rejection you'll get stronger and wiser. Don't let one "no" stop you from achieving your goal (remember the story of J. K. Rowling or the founder of KFC from Chapter 2.1?). Sometimes, you'll need to adjust the way you act and work. Sometimes you'll need to change your environment or your team. Sometimes you'll need to seek the advice of experts, adjust your comfort level, or update your skills. There's always something you can do to improve your chances of being accepted next time you try. It's like navigating to your destination—you never know which route is the fastest, the most wonderful, or the most convenient until you choose one, and then adapt if needed.

For example, if your goal is to speak at a top industry conference but your proposal gets rejected year after year— maybe you can first speak at another event or organise your own, even if it's only a live webinar. Maybe it's not the right time for you to appear in front of a huge audience, and it might be better to focus on extending your speaking experience first or keep coming up with new topics until your proposal is finally spot-on.

After every rejection, try to find out what you could do to get a "yes" in the future. The worst step you could take is to let negative thoughts and self-pity consume you. There will surely be many other opportunities for you to grow and reach your goals. A rejection may also mean that your time hasn't come yet. You can't succeed without putting yourself out there or taking a few risks. Sometimes all you need is just one "yes" after 99 "no's". So, take anything that goes against your plans as a valuable experience, identify any areas of improvement, and keep moving towards your goal with confidence. And if a rejection becomes too bitter to deal with, remember the times you've succeeded to get motivated again.

How can you manage your fear of rejection?
It's important to know how to behave when you hear "no", and also to learn to control your fear of rejection. In her book *Feel The Fear And Do It Anyway*, Susan Jeffers[7] explains that every fear can be reduced to one simple concern: "I won't be able to handle it." No matter whether it's rejection, failure, or criticism, it all boils down to this thought. We fear what we don't know, and we don't know how to behave if the improbable scenario becomes reality. In most cases, the only method to overcome your fear is to "do it anyway," to act despite your fear, to embrace your fear, accept it, and push through all the obstacles. If the thought of being rejected prevents you from moving

---

[7] Susan Jeffers, *Feel the Fear and Do It Anyway* (London: Vermilion, 2007).

forward with your business, there are some methods you can use to change your limiting beliefs.

Let go of the past

The fear of rejection—or any type of fear for that matter—may stem from painful events you experienced in the past. Maybe your ideas, offers, or suggestions were rejected at an earlier point and you took it very personally. Maybe this rejection was bundled with harsh criticism or mocking laughter. Such events can easily undermine your self-esteem and make you feel unworthy of success. The first step is to realise that your past doesn't determine your future. The previous rejections were not about you as a person. It was probably one idea, one offer, one proposal—not you or your business as a whole. Close that painful chapter and turn the page to start anew. Yes, I realise it's easier said than done, but sometimes our main obstacle is ourselves—our habits, our past, our thoughts. If you do your best to fully focus on the present moment, everything will become smoother. When you're focused on here and now, most fears lose their power.

Tell yourself a different story

Our mind is smart. It believes us. If you keep telling yourself a negative story, your mind will believe it's true. If you keep clinging to your fears, your mind will believe it's the only way to go. That's why a key step in fighting with your fears is to tell yourself a different story. For example, you can replace the memory of past painful events with a new image of yourself—one that shows that you're strong, fearless, and focused on victory. Use affirmations or visualisation to revive that image, and recall it every time you feel your power diminishing. Repeat to yourself several times per day that you deserve to close that dream deal, to earn that wonderful amount of money, to reach that magic number of clients/followers/reviews.

Shift your focus

Where your focus goes, the energy flows. With a new story about yourself, you'll be able to grow your immunity to fear and rejection. It will also help to get rid of negative words, both when speaking with others and with yourself. When you speak positively about other people, things and events, you'll start noticing that the world has more good than bad things to offer. There are more positives than negatives to you as well. All you need to do to realise it is to shift your focus away from the unlikely event of failure or rejection, and closer to the desired result.

Be in control

This might come as a surprise, but at the end of the day only you are responsible for your emotions. You can't blame the person next door who frowned at you, or your competitor who runs aggressive promotions—only you can control your feeling of envy, discomfort, distress, fear, or failure. No matter what causes your fear, it's an emotion like any other. It can be mastered. Once you identify your emotion, accept it, figure out what it is trying to tell you, and do your best to control it. For example, when you're terrified of giving a speech in front of a large audience, you can either let the fear paralyse your body, tie your tongue, turn your face purple, and cover your hands in sweat, or you can simply breathe through this initially uncomfortable emotion. Even if that means asking your audience for a short pause so that you can have a sip of water, sit down, and collect your thoughts (real-life story!).

Sooner or later in your freelance career you'll have to accept not being accepted. Rejection is a constant part of every freelancer's life. There's nothing wrong with you if your offers, proposals, or ideas get turned down from time to time. Behind every rejection is a valuable experience that can motivate you and inspire you to act in a totally new way. The key to success is to learn to deal with a "no" and use it to your advantage.

Frontline stories: how I befriended my fear of rejection

Looking back at my freelance career, I could probably find more "rejection stories" than "acceptance stories". From the simple fear of: "What if I decline to work on that project and the customer never comes back?" to the more complicated: "What if I take a short break and my customers won't work with me again?" to the most painful: "What if I take maternity leave from my solopreneurship and my clients won't wait until I'm back?" In most cases, these scary scenarios didn't come true at all. But there were other rejections: project quotes that weren't accepted, collaboration applications with what I thought would be my perfect client that were turned down, courses that never reached my desired sales numbers, side hustles I undertook with my husband that didn't work out or public-speaking proposals that weren't approved. I even followed in the footsteps of J.K. Rowling and had my first Polish novel rejected or unnoticed by 30 publishers. Although painful at first, all these rejections made me more immune to any potential "no's". I learned my lesson: it's not always about me. There are so many other reasons for being turned down. In the case of the book, publishers choose what they think will sell, and they receive thousands of proposals every single day. Their silence doesn't mean my book is unreadable. In the case of missed collaboration opportunities, maybe my dream clients decided to work with a partner that was recommended by their trusted colleagues. Their rejection doesn't mean my services aren't good enough. We simply weren't the right match for each other. I figured out that out of 100 attempts at anything I do, only 1% will work out, so with time I learned to focus on that 1% through affirmation, visualisation, and by eliminating any negative self-talk.

2.4 Impostor syndrome

Would you dare to call yourself an expert if you were rejected from multiple jobs over a period of 12 months? It takes an enormous superpower to believe in your skills regardless of what other people say. It requires tremendous courage to create your own workplace when no one wants you. That's exactly what Ellen Mackenzie did when she started her own side hustle as a social media manager while being employed as a journalist. Before she could quit her nine-to-five position and become a successful founder of Dishing Up Digital, she had to boost her confidence and erase the phrase "I'm not good enough" from her vocabulary. In her podcast, she describes how during a call with a potential new client she was referred to as an "expert", but her immediate thought was "I'm not an expert at all." Luckily, she didn't vocalise her doubts, the call went on, and eventually she booked a new client. When she realised that her customers believed in her competence more than she did, Ellen embarked on a mission to get rid of her self-doubt.[8]

Impostor syndrome affects nearly 70% of people at some point of their lives.[9] It describes a thought pattern where a person constantly fears being exposed as a fraud. This condition often affects high-achieving individuals who are perceived as successful but don't internalise their accomplishments. Typical symptoms include self-doubt and feelings of not being good enough or not good at a particular task.

Usually, people suffering from this phenomenon associate their success with sheer luck, not with their actual skills. Initially, this symptom was only attributed to high-achieving professional women,[10] but studies have since found that anyone can experience feelings of inadequacy, especially those from minority ethnic or racial groups.[11]

It may come as a surprise that many popular entrepreneurs, athletes, actors, or singers admit that they have struggled with impostor syndrome. In one of her interviews, Jennifer Lopez revealed: "Even though I had sold 70 million albums, there I was feeling like, I'm no good at this." Meryl Streep doubted that anyone would want to see her in another movie, saying: "I don't know how to act anyway, so why am I doing this?"[12] Arianna Huffington was convinced that her non-native English would make people reject her ideas,[13] both Michelle Obama and Sheryl Sandberg admit in their books[14,15] that they often felt "not good enough" in their professional careers. So, if you also doubt your professional skills or you're convinced that you're a fraud, you're not alone. In fact, you're in great

---

[8] "How Imposter Syndrome Is Robbing You" (Dishing Up Digital with Ellen Mackenzie, 2021), https://www.ellenmackenzie.com/podcasts/dishing-up-digital-with-ellen-mackenzie/episodes/2147558501.

[9] Jaruwan Sakulku, "The Impostor Phenomenon". *The Journal of Behavioral Science* 6, no.1 (2011): pp. 75-97. https://doi.org/10.14456/ijbs.2011.6.

[10] Pauline Rose Clance, *The Impostor Phenomenon: When Success Makes You Feel like a Fake* (Atlanta: Peachtree Publishers, 1985).

[11] Joan C. Harvey and Cynthia Katz, *If I'm so Successful, Why Do I Feel like a Fake?: The Imposter Phenomenon* (New York: St Martins Pr, 1985).

[12] Marie Claire, "16 Celebrity Quotes on Suffering with Impostor Syndrome," Marie Claire UK, November 10, 2016, https://www.marieclaire.co.uk/entertainment/celebrity-quotes-on-impostor-syndrome-434739.

[13] Krista Gray, "4 Successful People Share How They Triumphed over Imposter Syndrome, the Belief That You'll Be Exposed as a 'Fraud'," Business Insider (Business Insider, January 15, 2019), https://www.businessinsider.com/how-to-overcome-imposter-syndrome-2019-1.

[14] Michelle Obama, *Becoming* (New York: Crown, 2018).

[15] Sheryl Sandberg and Akiko Murai, *Lean In: Women, Work, and the Will to Lead* (New York: Alfred A. Knopf, 2013).

company. Whether you've just hit your first five-figure month or booked your dream client—something in the back of your head might be telling you that you don't deserve it. "I was lucky"—that's your automatic reply when someone congratulates you on being selected as the best business owner in your town, being invited to speak at the biggest conference in your industry, or having your website featured on a major design platform. Of course, "good luck" plays an important role in business life, but ultimately, your achievements can be attributed mainly to your performance. Now you might be wondering: "What about connections? Being in the right place in the right time?" Yes, these factors matter, but aren't they related to your skills as well? After all, would you be able to make the right connections and remain memorable if it wasn't for who you are and what you do? Would you know how to use the golden "right time, right place" opportunity if you didn't have your unique set of skills? Your performance is the key.

All the successful people mentioned earlier eventually learned to conquer their impostor syndrome or at least managed to keep moving forward despite their self-doubt. You too can follow in their footsteps. There are many strategies that you can adopt to eliminate impostor syndrome from your business life.

Become a member of a supportive community
Joining a positive community will help you create a feeling of belonging. Impostor syndrome often surfaces when we feel misaligned. Imagine you're going to your first industry conference at a huge hotel with thousands of people who seem to be at ease (that's exactly what happened to me!), or you end up in a new business environment and have to work in your fancy client's location—these situations may trigger your self-

doubt or overwhelm you. A supportive group will help you balance that discomfort. This can be a professional association, sports club, religious centre, neighbourhood association, or simply a small group of trusted friends. Meeting with them regularly, being active, helping other members, sharing your thoughts, and talking about your uncomfortable moments and your concerns will allow you to create a counterbalance to your doubts. It will boost your self-confidence and encourage you to act, even if you feel inadequate. Every time imposter syndrome creeps in, you can revive that comfortable atmosphere, think about the encouraging words you heard from your friends, and recall what it means to be completely accepted.

My supportive group turned out to be my ashtanga yoga community. Even if we didn't talk about our professional lives, somehow the friendly atmosphere and the feeling of being accepted for who I am kept spreading to all other areas of my daily life. Before the coronavirus pandemic, when my city hosted conferences, meet-ups and networking events, I would run to a fancy business location nearly every single day straight after my morning ashtanga practise to immerse myself into a totally different world. Of course, there were moments when I felt awkward among so many marketers, developers, IT specialists, gamers, or self-proclaimed influencers, but the morning dose of "belonging" helped me to push my concerns into the background. That's how I learned that being a member of a supportive community can keep reminding you about your superpowers and help you bounce back whenever you start to doubt your skills.

Keep a success log

If you love journaling, a success log might be an effective tool to help you cherish your achievements and remind you about your strengths whenever doubts paralyse you. All you need to do is to write down any positive feedback that you receive from your customers, colleagues, or business partners, describe moments that made you feel proud, and highlight all the goals that you achieved. Be meticulous. Every situation, goal, and achievement counts, no matter how small. Even a short comment like "Great job" typed by your customer in your e-mail exchange can be powerful enough to deserve a place in your success log. If your website has a section with testimonials, you can copy positive online reviews to your log as well. Your LinkedIn recommendations should be there too. After a while, your success log will become an impressive mirror of your past accomplishments. Whenever you feel inadequate, not smart enough, not skilled enough, or not successful enough, you can grab your success log to find your confidence again.

Ask for feedback

How you see yourself is not how others perceive you. You may doubt your skills, but perhaps your colleagues are impressed with your expertise. You may feel like a misfit, but your business partners could appreciate your flexibility and open-mindedness. You'll probably never find out what other people think about you unless you ask. How can you do this in a non-aggressive way? This will depend on your and your colleagues' communication culture. If you're afraid to ask a direct question about your performance, you can send an invitation to a short online survey about your services or ask your clients to fill in a short questionnaire about their experience working with you. You can also reformulate your request and use phrases such as "Is there anything you'd like to improve in our collaboration?", "What do you like the most about working with me?", or "Do you think you were able to solve your problem by collaborating with me?" For some people, these questions will be more encouraging than a simple "What do you think about my work?" Of course, not all answers you receive will be positive, so get ready for less enthusiastic feedback as well. Even if you learn that your customer was unsatisfied with your work, at least you'll find out what to improve. Feedback is a great tool for a quick reality check, but it will only be useful if you're ready to accept both the good and the bad news.

Share your knowledge
Probably the worst step to take when you're fighting with impostor syndrome is to contain it within you. Succumbing to that vicious voice that keeps saying you're a fraud is like falling into a black hole. There's no way out. So, before you get sucked into that void, find out how you can serve others. How can your "not-enough-ness" become illuminating for someone else? Even if you doubt your skills, there must be something you're really good at, or at least better at than the majority of your colleagues, friends, and competitors. You don't have to jump straight into public speaking, there are other ways to pass on your wisdom. You can share tips on social media, create a podcast, write a blog, publish an e-book, or get featured in an interview in a popular podcast or magazine in your industry. There are many ways to share your wisdom. Maybe your knowledge seems obvious to you, but for others it might be life changing.

When I was about to give my first public speech, I was convinced that my content was so basic and non-revolutionary that my audience would roll their eyes and leave the room. Of course, that didn't happen. On the contrary, I made them smile, opened their eyes to some common problems in software localisation, and eventually received positive feedback. However, the thought that what I'm sharing is obvious is nearly always somewhere in the back of my mind, whether I'm writing a short post on social media, working on a long article, preparing a speech for a conference, or writing a book (this one too!). But the only way to refute that thought is to go out into the world, say what you want to say out loud, and wait for a response. Nearly every time, it will be surprisingly comforting.

You too can inspire others to achieve more, help them solve a difficult problem, or shed more light on a complex issue. Once you start sharing your knowledge, be it in a formal or informal way, your focus will shift. Your thoughts won't revolve around yourself and how you're perceived by others. Instead, you'll focus on your audience, readers, listeners, or followers. By helping others, you'll help yourself as well, and your impostor syndrome will start losing its grip on you.

Be honest

Honesty is the best policy. Why not tell your trusted colleagues or close friends about your impostor syndrome? Once you bring up that topic, you'll probably hear stories similar to yours. "That's exactly how I feel too!" or "Don't worry, I constantly think people will find out that I don't know as much as they think I do," or "I don't think I'm qualified enough either." Chances are people around you will react with similar words. Try to name your feelings, discuss the methods each of you use to overcome impostor syndrome, and figure out how to support others. Maybe someone will suggest affirmations, visualisations, or practicing gratitude. Someone else will argue that none of these methods work, and someone will claim that only a therapist can help. All opinions are equally valuable; what matters is that you and your friends or colleagues can openly talk about your experiences with imposter syndrome. It's reassuring to know that you're not the only person who feels inadequate.

Understand your triggers
Do you know what triggers imposter syndrome for you? What situations, environments, words, activities, or types of people make you feel inadequate? Maybe you feel like you're not enough when you scroll your social media timeline overloaded with happy and successful people sharing only their happy and successful moments? Maybe it happens when you take on new roles, join new teams, meet new clients, or network with new groups of people? Maybe your biggest trigger is comparing yourself to others? Try to understand your triggers and the emotions associated with them. In this way, you'll be able to gain more control and either avoid behaviour that causes your imposter syndrome (such as playing the comparison game) or prepare to act with more confidence in uncomfortable situations (such as talking to new clients).

Get a coach
If your impostor syndrome seems to be out of control and you constantly fear being exposed as a fraud, it's time to get professional help. Find a coach or therapist that will help you unlock your potential and overcome any barriers that might be related to your past experiences. For example, your impostor

syndrome might be related to your need to protect yourself for some reason, or it may stem from the fear that no one will accept the "real you". With the help of a therapist, you'll be able to understand where your self-doubt and limiting thoughts come from, as well as how to accept and embrace them. Once you find a safe space to express your feelings, you'll be able to increase your confidence and realise that you deserve to be successful, even if you're constantly in the process of getting better.

The key to success in overcoming impostor syndrome is to shift your focus from "I don't know how" and "I'm not good enough" to "I'm on the journey to become my best self." It's easier said than done, but with little changes in your routine, such as writing in your success log daily or having regular conversations with a trusted person, you'll be able to grow your confidence and avoid negative thinking patterns.

2.5 Perfectionism

Impostor syndrome is closely related to another obstacle: perfectionism. Perfectionists set excessively high goals, strive for flawlessness, and tend to be overly critical of themselves or others. Some even take it to another level by becoming control freaks who micromanage every single aspect of their work, even if they have team members, partners, or colleagues who could easily take over their tasks. I'm sure you've met many perfectionists in your life. Maybe you work with one, maybe you live with one under the same roof, or maybe you're a perfectionist yourself. All these scenarios can be equally frustrating. It's hard to work with someone who requires 100% perfect results, 100% of the time. Collaboration becomes cumbersome when your partners can't delegate tasks or when they're never satisfied with any achievement, believing the project could have been done better. When a perfectionist ends up working with a realist, their worlds collide. Eventually, the mutual frustration builds up and both parties decide they're better off alone. I've experienced this first-hand: I live and work with a perfectionist.

How can you find common ground when you collaborate with people who aren't like you? And, more importantly, how can you make sure perfectionism doesn't become an obstacle to your success? Let's first have a look at the pitfalls of being a perfectionist.

Achieving less by stressing more

The main problem with being a perfectionist is that you're likely to achieve less by stressing more as compared to regular high achievers.[16] Although sometimes perfectionism helps to achieve better results, in most cases it's a serious obstacle in moving forward. Unhealthy perfectionism can lead to procrastination, constant lack of satisfaction, fear of being criticised for mistakes, and overly controlling behaviour. This in turn causes stress and impacts personal relationships, which can ultimately lead to burnout, depression, low self-esteem, or sleep disturbances.[17] Your mental and physical health are at stake when your perfectionist mind runs wild. Luckily, there are proven methods to take control of your perfectionist behaviour and avoid all these negative effects.

Progress instead of perfection

With your busy freelancer's schedule, you probably won't be able to complete every single business activity to the highest possible standard. Add to that housework, social life, family responsibilities, or physical activity, and daily life will quickly become too complex to manage. There's simply not enough time in a day to perfect every single detail. Perfectionism can stop you from trying out new things and make you procrastinate on your work and ideas (more about that in the next chapter).

---

[16] Brian Swider et al., "The Pros and Cons of Perfectionism, According to Research," Harvard Business Review, December 27, 2018, https://hbr.org/2018/12/the-pros-and-cons-of-perfectionism-according-to-research.

[17] Pelin Kanten and Murat Yesıltas, "The Effects of Positive and Negative Perfectionism on Work Engagement, Psychological Well-Being and Emotional Exhaustion," *Procedia Economics and Finance* 23 (2015): pp. 1367-1375, https://doi.org/10.1016/s2212-5671(15)00522-5.

Instead of aiming for perfection, focus on progress. For example, keeping to deadlines agreed with your customers probably plays a key role in your business. If your client asks you to create a project proposal by Thursday, submitting a perfect copy on Friday won't be better than a good enough version delivered on time. You'll need to define your priorities, set realistic goals, and get used to trade-offs. Good enough is sometimes good enough—you can't be perfect in all circumstances and in all roles that life forces you to take on. But you can shift your focus to progress. With this mindset, mistakes don't equal failure. Instead, they give you a reason to keep learning and evolving. What matters is the bigger picture: meeting deadlines and making sure that your customers are happy and your business is growing.

Start where you are now
Sometimes you really need to begin your journey somewhere without waiting for the perfect conditions. You can start your project or work on your business idea with what you have now, then tweak and adjust it along the way. Let's assume you want to create an online course to generate more income streams. Your content is ready, but you're fixated on the ideal format and presentation. To achieve your dream result, you're convinced that you'll first need to invest in expensive equipment, develop superb video-editing skills, and find a breath-taking location to shoot your course. You don't have any of these things yet, so you keep waiting for all the pieces of the puzzle to fall into place. After six months spent on preparations, your course is still on your to-do list, while other entrepreneurs grab the opportunity and produce content on a similar topic without any fancy locations or top-notch equipment. Your time

is your money, so sometimes you'll need to accept a reasonable compromise. If you're inspired and feel you can inspire your students, maybe releasing the course in a not-so-perfect format isn't such a bad idea. You can always improve the published material or tweak it later during the maintenance process. In most cases, done is better than perfect, so try not to spend a lot of time on every task just to make it a little bit better. Ask yourself these simple questions: Is focusing on every little detail really worth it? What am I trying to achieve? Are these details essential to reach my goal?

Apply the 80/20 rule

Did you know that 80% of your outcomes come from 20% of your inputs? If you continue working on something to achieve 100% perfection, you might be using your time and energy in an inefficient way. For example, I could write a decent blog article in one hour. But I could also spend three more hours on trying to reformulate my wording, finding better idioms, coming up with more engaging examples, adding more sources and statistics, or being overly picky with style and grammar. Of course, all these steps might be essential, but only the first hour spent on my work (the magical 20%) helped me achieve the essence of my article. If I continue tweaking and adjusting my text to achieve 100% perfection, I might end up wasting extra hours, days, or even weeks and still not consider my work completed. By using the 80/20 rule you can focus on the results that are good enough. This means delivering tasks that are 80% perfect because working on that extra 20% wouldn't add much to the overall picture.

I've seen this rule being applied in many industries for various tasks, for example, in software testing. There's a reason professional testers claim that complete testing is impossible. One issue is that it's almost impossible to test for all use cases, all possible inputs, or all possible execution environments, especially when the software system depends on the outside world, such as weather, temperature, or pressure. That's why tests are usually carried out based on the test script and for a limited number of test rounds. When I used to work on localisation testing projects, the rule of thumb was to run only two rounds of tests. Of course, you can't detect all issues in this way, but at least you can make sure that the product is "good enough". Thus, the magic 80% will be achieved, and there's no point to test further to perfect the remaining 20%. Plus, in most cases, users send feedback to developers, so any further bugs can be repaired with software updates.

If you're struggling with your perfectionist tendencies, you can remind yourself every single day: "Good enough is good enough." Especially if the task you're working on is not on your list of top priorities. To define your priorities—areas where you're "allowed" to deliver 100% perfection—you can follow the advice of Dr. Jeff Szymanski, a clinical psychologist and author of *The Perfectionist's Handbook*.[18] He recommends identifying four categories of tasks: "A tasks", which include work skills or tasks at which you would like to excel, "B tasks", meaning all the tasks where you can give your 80%, "C tasks" that no one perceives as significant, meaning that you can easily

---

[18] Jeff Szymanski, *The Perfectionist's Handbook: Take Risks, Invite Criticism, and Make the Most of Your Mistakes* (New Jersey: Harvard Health Publications, 2011).

lower the bar and be only average at them, and finally "F tasks" that are very time-consuming and in reality don't matter at all. Such tasks don't bring you any satisfaction, and they don't garner any recognition either. While categorising your tasks, don't get carried away and select only three items in each category. Once you complete your classification process, you'll know where to put your 100%, where you can be only good enough (80%), where to allow yourself to be mediocre, and what to ignore. This approach will allow you to focus on what really matters, helping to avoid burnout, stress, or exhaustion.

Learn to delegate

Delegating tasks is a difficult undertaking for many business owners, even if you're not a perfectionist. That has definitely been the case for me for many long years. I preferred to do everything by myself—from administration, marketing, client acquisition, to actual project delivery. Not because of the fees that the experts in each of these fields demand (although this issue played a big role at the beginning of my freelancing career), but mainly out of conviction that no one would understand my business and my ideas as deeply as I did. I knew I could create my own website, so why would I outsource it to a designer? I could run my social media campaigns, so why would I ask a marketer to help me? I could do my own tax filing, so why hire an expert? This game was going on and on in my head until the day became too short to work both *on* my business and *in* my business. When I noticed that walking outside of my home office started feeling like I was hovering in a virtual reality, I knew it was time to cut down my working hours and hire specialists for the tasks that were too time-consuming or weren't my strong points. The first step was to hire a professional accountant. Although his rates weren't low,

I was relieved that I could finally spend more time translating and less time stressing about taxes and administration. Although this step might seem straightforward, it did require some degree of courage and open-mindedness from my side. With time, I learned to trust other people, and slowly my "I can do it all on my own" attitude began to disappear.

For a perfectionist, delegating tasks is even more challenging than it is for control freaks or people with trust issues. Once you define your A, B, C, and F tasks, you'll realise which projects in your business could be assigned to someone else. Do you really need to clean your own yoga studio after hours of teaching and practising with your students? Do you really have to spend two hours per day on managing your business's social profiles? Maybe someone else could take over this task to let you focus on your core business activity. By delegating, you can make space to excel at your A tasks. At the same time, you let others perform their A tasks with 100% outcome. But what if the results aren't up to your standards? Well, every partnership needs some tweaking at the beginning. You can ask your colleague to correct the little imperfections, and worst-case scenario, you can find a replacement. I have seen my perfectionist husband struggling with this scenario many times, but even if he had to ask his colleague to tweak the details of a project or if he was forced to replace the sloppy collaborator with a skilled expert, he still appreciated the benefits of outsourcing his C or F tasks to others. Yes, delegating will cost you some money, but you'll gain the only thing you can't buy: time. Your mental and physical health will also benefit tremendously.

How to work with a perfectionist
(or anyone who is not like you)

Perfectionism may also become a major hurdle even when you're not the one displaying this kind of behaviour. You may end up working with team members who are overly perfectionist, which complicates and slows down the whole project in your view. Working with people driven by perfection used to be one of my biggest stumbling blocks. I used to push them to deliver their tasks, but they would only pull back and ask for more time to ensure that every detail was top-notch. Although there's nothing wrong with being detail-focused, sometimes you need to accept results that are good enough to avoid perpetual deadline extensions. My perfectionist colleagues wouldn't agree that done is better than perfect, so there was constant tension. Until I learned to adopt their point of view.

If you also struggle to find a balance when working with people who are not like you, here are some key steps that can help you ensure a smooth collaboration:

Focus on what you have in common

Whether the problem is a clash between different personality types, cultural backgrounds, or skill sets, you can always find common ground to make your relationship healthy. Maybe you both have the same goals, maybe you're both eager to complete the project on time, or maybe you're both motivated to serve your customers in the best possible way. Find out what you and your partner want to achieve as a team, not as individuals. This is the first step to shift your focus from your differences and place it on what really matters. It may also help to define the priorities in every project. For example, sometimes meeting a deadline will be a non-negotiable requirement, and sometimes the budget will play a key role. As long as your partner's perfectionist tendencies don't prevent you from fulfilling the project's key requirements, you can let them tweak the details as long as they want. In other cases, keep reminding your colleagues that time is of the essence and that they should meet the deadline, even if the results are only good enough.

Adopt a growth mindset
Once you find common ground, it's time to adapt to your partner. Waiting for your colleague to change will only lead to frustration. Instead, adjust your own style. Try to understand your colleague who acts in a too logical or too detailed way. That person who constantly asks for more time probably doesn't do it to delay your project on purpose, but prefers to research a task thoroughly to ensure that they deliver high-quality work. Maybe your partner is pushy with her ideas because she is emotionally attached to her work. Try to read between the lines, and don't let emotions influence your behaviour. Act with respect and courtesy, focusing on your colleague's strengths. If your perfectionist partner is testing your patience, withdraw and regroup before you burst with frustration. You can gently remind your partner that not all details are equally important. This approach will help you learn more from each other and increase the chances for successful collaboration.

Communicate clearly
Most tensions arise because of a lack of communication. Maybe your partner has different assumptions, maybe your message wasn't clear enough, or maybe it didn't reach your colleague on time. When you recognise perfectionist

tendencies in your colleagues, pay special attention to the instructions they give you. Recap your discussions, follow up, and double-check if anything is ambiguous. Clear communication is key to success, especially if you collaborate with people with different work styles, expertise, or with very specific expectations. Always confirm via e-mail what you have agreed on in your conversations, and make sure your partner has no doubts about the project requirements and plan. This will help you avoid misunderstandings, missed deadlines, and lost opportunities. Agree up-front how many corrections you'll implement if your perfectionist partner is unhappy with your work. Otherwise, you'll end up tweaking your code or polishing your text without end because your partner will always claim that something is lacking.

It may come as a surprise to you, but working with perfectionists (or anyone who isn't like you) may help you to become more flexible, creative, and open-minded. Having a perfectionist in my team (and in my house) taught me how to control my emotions and focus on common goals. Instead of bursting with anger and complaining about time wasted on unnecessary details, I keep asking questions: Do we really need that? Is there any other way to achieve this? Are you sure these details are all that important? Sometimes, my perfectionist colleagues will pause for a moment and realise that a good enough result might also be satisfactory. Sometimes, they will frown at me and claim that their task has to be 100% perfect for the project to succeed. In most cases, they're right. That perfectly executed task usually impresses our customers and keeps them coming back. But who knows, maybe the customer would still be satisfied if our perfectionist only gave 80 or 90%

of their effort... It's all about finding the right balance. Remaining calm and open to your business partner's suggestions will definitely help to overcome any differences.

2.6 Procrastination

While a perfectionist thinks "Why would I do it if I can overdo it?", a procrastinator answers with: "Why would I do it today if I can do it tomorrow?" There's always a good excuse to reschedule, postpone, delay, or abandon a planned activity: unfavourable weather, bad mood, stars that don't align. For a procrastinator, every excuse is reasonable.

If memes and the Internet were a common thing in the early 90s, the most popular phrase (at least among my peers and in my region) would probably have been: "What you were going to do today, do tomorrow instead...then you gain two days off." For better or worse, the Internet was still in its infancy back then, so instead of making it as an Internet meme, this phrase conquered posters, postcards, and t-shirts. My friends at school would show off with their slacker's approach, continuously repeating that they are not in a hurry, that they can easily leave everything to the last minute and still manage to study for a test, do their homework, or complete a lousy housekeeping task assigned by their parents. My answer to all these statements, although usually only in my head, was: "But why?" The procrastination trend was beyond my comprehension. One day, probably just for fun, my mum printed an image with the "Gain two days off" phrase and put it on my desk. Mind you, this was in the early 90s, so even printing in a little town in Poland was quite an undertaking (although we did have a massive PC and an Internet connection, which made us technology pioneers in our little town at that time). Confused, I looked at the image with the wonky words. How was that supposed to help me? I was tempted to cross out the words "today" and "tomorrow" and switch them around. Such an approach made more sense to me. Why would I do something tomorrow if I could do it today? I could rest once I ticked everything off my list. In this way I would still gain "two days off," or was I missing something? The idea of leaving things for later still baffles me today.

In my early teenage years, I would start studying for a test at least one week in advance, dividing the big chunk of material into doable steps. For example, I would study one chapter per day for three days, then on day four, I would repeat everything I had learned, then study the next two chapters for two days and revise everything on day seven. I loved coming up with different study systems ahead of time. Procrastination was out of the question. This attitude followed me for the rest of my life, which often caused misunderstandings among my friends, colleagues, and family members. For some reason, I've always been surrounded by people who love to delay their tasks until the last minute, which obviously irritates me, to put it mildly. What's worse is that I even ended up marrying a perfectionist procrastinator, which was probably a gift from heaven in that it forced me to balance my anti-procrastination and anti-perfectionism tendencies.

Unlike my fears of rejection, failure, and criticism, my experience with procrastination hasn't been an obstacle that I've had to overcome to run my business. However, as my private and professional paths crossed with hardcore procrastinators multiple times, I ended up being that person in the room who always tried to explain that a proactive approach might be more effective. If you suspect procrastination might be one of the barriers to growing your freelance business, try experimenting with these proven methods:

Start before you're ready

That's probably the worst advice one could give to a procrastinator. But it's also the most effective solution. To stop putting off your tasks, you need to change your thought patterns. Quit overthinking. Give up the idea that everything has to be 100% ready before you make a call, launch a new project, contact a new client, or run a marketing campaign. While perfectionists have to forget about delivering projects that are 100% perfect and learn that sometimes 80% is more than enough, they also have to realise that being 100% ready is a myth. Again, 80% is equally fine. Whether you feel paralysed by a number of variables that have to be in the right place before you start or you're overwhelmed by the number of choices you're offered—there's only one solution: take the first step. As Marc Randolph said in the Marie Forleo Podcast,[19] every idea is stupid, but you won't know that until you start converting it into action, tweaking and adjusting it to convert it into success. His idea of creating a subscription platform for streaming services was heavily criticised. Even his mother claimed such a service would be a failure. But instead of waiting for some magical nod of approval from the universe, he simply started toying with his idea until Netflix was born. He wasn't ready when he started converting his plan into reality, and he didn't have the necessary knowledge and skills. But during the process, he was tweaking, adjusting, and testing new waters to make his vision come true. Of course, Marc Randolph is not the only entrepreneur who took action without waiting to be 100% ready. In fact, most successful

---

[19] Marie Forleo, "This Netflix Co-Founder Turned His Idea Into A Company Worth Over $100 Billion | Marc Randolph," Marieforleo.com, June 7, 2022, https://www.marieforleo.com/blog/marc-randolph-netflix.

businesspeople admit that they took the first step without being completely prepared. One action propelled another, one meeting led to another, and so with time, they collected all the pieces of their success puzzles. It took only one decision, one small step to set off in the right direction, even though the road was foggy.

Your vision doesn't have to be as big as creating another Netflix, but it's still wise to approach your plan with more self-awareness. Whenever you're stuck in the analysis-paralysis mode, unable to make any decisions and progress with your task, step back and ask yourself: What am I trying to achieve? Do I really need to have control over all variables? Is it really so important to have every step carefully mapped out? Maybe I can trust my intuition, learn by doing, constantly tweaking and fine-tuning my ideas.

Starting before you feel fully prepared may help you avoid many headaches and sleepless nights. It will also save you time and effort. The first step is what matters the most. You can always stop for a while, take a step back, and then start running forward again.

Break your tasks into smaller pieces
Another way to escape the trap of procrastination is to divide your plan into smaller, less overwhelming tasks. Imagine your goal is to open an online store with ethnic decoration. You've identified a niche in the market, and your research clearly shows that there's demand for such products in your region. You also happen to be passionate about ethnic design, so such a line of business would be perfectly suited for you. There's

only one major doubt that stops you from acting on your idea: You know nothing about running an online store. The whole process, from acquiring great products to presenting them online and eventually making the first sale, seems terribly complex. That's why you keep procrastinating, waiting to learn more about e-commerce or online marketing. What about breaking your big, complex idea into smaller bits? For example, you could start by completing some courses on e-commerce technology, consult with specialists in this field, or talk to successful e-store owners. You could also ask for recommendations to find the best way to sell your products, find a website developer, or learn how to create a website by yourself based on a template (for example, Shopify). Your e-store doesn't have to be ready in one day, but there are small things you can do every day to move closer to your goal, even if it's as simple as reading a blog article about effective e-store marketing strategies.

No matter what you're planning to accomplish, breaking your plan into smaller, doable pieces will help you find more motivation to keep going. If your to-do list reads, "Create a web store," you'll be much more overwhelmed compared to if you simply write, "Contact three developers to ask for rates and timelines." Make it easy on yourself by dividing big ideas into the tiniest possible steps. In this way, you'll be slowly moving forward instead of being stuck in one place, unable to make any decisions.

Eliminate distractions
The best way to find out what will help you overcome your procrastination habits is probably talking to other procrastinators who have been on the same journey. Well, as

you might have guessed already, I'm anything but a procrastinator, so in my mission to learn more about a procrastinating mind, I've engaged in long discussions with those who procrastinate regularly. That was an easy task, as for some reason, destiny sent me friends and family who adore delaying and putting off their plans. In any case, I did my best to understand why they tend to reschedule everything for tomorrow. One of the most common replies was: "There are so many other, more interesting things to do." Simply put, there are too many distractions. When both the online world and real life have so much to offer, it's easy to fall down the rabbit hole. You only want to read one article to help you prepare for your presentation, but one click leads to another, and another, until you realise you've just spent two hours mindlessly browsing the Web. Yes, there are many opportunities to explore, connect, or boost your skills. There might also be many tasks that need your attention, especially when you work from home and your business life is constantly intertwined with your family responsibilities. But you need to learn to set limits. Define your boundaries. Create your to-do list and stick to it. Eliminate distractions. But how?

First, turn off all phone notifications and close your social media platforms when it's time to work. If you use social media to work, schedule certain times during the day when you'll only focus on social media marketing, scheduling your posts, or connecting with your community. Next, make sure your workspace is as minimal as possible. Declutter it, remove all empty dishes, crumbs, or sheets of paper piling up in front of you. A tidy and clean workspace will put your mind at ease. On the other hand, a disorganised desk will make your brain chaotic and unable to focus, which is a shortcut to procrastination. If you don't have a spare room to use as your home office and your only option is to work in a designated corner of another room, make sure it's not your bedroom. Your mind will automatically switch to rest and relaxation in the bedroom, making it more challenging to work productively. Also, when you later go to bed in that room, you might have problems falling asleep. If these methods aren't effective enough and you still struggle to keep your wandering mind on track, it's time to refocus. Write down your disruptive thoughts and ideas, then come back to your to-do list. If another great plan comes to mind while you work, don't jump to a new task immediately. Again, put it down on paper, schedule it for later, and return to the task at hand. Controlling our monkey minds is not an easy endeavour, but with some extra effort you can learn to tame it. Once you complete one task, reward yourself with a few minutes of daydreaming or mindless browsing, but set an alarm clock to remind yourself when it's time to get back to work.

Sometimes, no matter what you do, you won't be able to get into work mode. To flip the switch, try dropping the task you're stuck on and start somewhere else. For example, if you design or write in a linear way, move a few steps forward and work on another bit of your project. Then come back to where you left off to edit the challenging piece. Don't put it off for tomorrow just because you don't know how to finish one paragraph. Great ideas come in the least expected moments, usually when we don't force ourselves to find inspiration. For example, when I was writing my first book, the best concepts would pop into my mind while I was breastfeeding my daughter or practising yoga. As I'm writing this book I'm not breastfeeding anymore, but the best ideas still pop into my head while I'm doing routine tasks. That's when my mind is not distracted by social media, e-mails, or tempting offers. So, in your journey toward a focused mind, learn to identify and eliminate your distractions to design a healthy space in which you can work, create, and thrive.

Reward yourself for your accomplishments

I've just confessed to you that I never procrastinate. Well, that isn't entirely true. Sometimes I might be caught red-handed scrolling mindlessly through social media. One day I took a quick break from a technical translation project to unburden my brain. I did this by checking my Instagram account. Nothing really new was going on there that day: pictures of people doing asanas, business motivation quotes, images of busy working mums, people dancing in front of their screens. The same content, but in a different edition. Then my attention was drawn to a short video of a lady boasting about how much she had on her to-do list but there was no way she would start working on her tasks. I was appalled. Even more so when I checked her tagline and realised she was a business coach. Seriously? Would I follow, hire, or take advice from someone who shows off with this kind of approach? And then I reflected on my own actions. I was doing exactly the same thing, just without telling the whole world about it. Within an instant, I closed Instagram and went back to my project. Soon after that, I established my reward system. Any time I'd finish a challenging task or part of an assignment, I would allow myself five to 10 minutes of socialising, browsing topics that interest me, or reading inspiring articles. This attitude has proven to also be effective for procrastinators. If you can't force yourself to start ticking off the items on your to-do list, plan short rewards after every important step. Drinking coffee in the garden, going for a quick walk, talking to someone working next to you, or checking your social media—it could be anything as long as you set clear rules and stick to them. Define when you're allowed to take a break, for example after an hour of intense work or once you finish a task. Then decide how long you can indulge in your rewarding activity without breaking your momentum or feeling demotivated. With an efficient reward system, you'll be more likely to tame your procrastinating mind and get more things done.

Focus on your goals instead of on your tasks

This might sound a bit contradictory to what I've said earlier. You've just read that moving from one task to another can help to decrease the likelihood of procrastinating, and now here I am telling you to focus on the big goals instead of small tasks. Well, these are not necessarily conflicting ideas. Having your finish line in mind will motivate you to put more effort into all the little tasks you need to complete to reach your goal. For example, if you're working on a new website, you might break your project into several steps such as booking a domain name and hosting, searching for a decent template, installing it, and modifying the layout. When one of the tasks seems too overwhelming, consider it as part of the bigger picture: perceive it as a vehicle to your amazing website. Visualise your end product while working on every single step to remind yourself about the purpose of your work. This approach might help you avoid postponing individual steps because you'll realise how essential every phase is. You can't skip the tedious job of choosing images for the website if your goal is to impress your visitors with unique visuals, and you can't delay writing engaging copy if you want to amaze your readers. Looking *through* the tasks instead of *at* the tasks forces you to find those last waves of energy and motivation to finish your project on time.

This approach reminds me of one helpful exercise I had to complete as an 18-year-old girl during a self-defence course for women. Apart from all the empowerment talks I heard and efficient physical defence techniques I had to practise, this course taught me one more important strategy: nothing is too difficult if you look past it. To put this method into action, at the end of the two-day course we had to break a block of wood with one punch. The trick was to look through it and avoid focusing on the wood itself. Only then would it be possible to break the wood into pieces. This is what the teacher claimed as she showed us how to destroy the block with one hit. "It's very easy"—she said—"simply imagine that your hand goes through the wood." And so, I did. I moved my arm up, looked through the wood instead of at the wood, and bam! My first ever punch was surprisingly successful. I still have those two pieces of wood in my apartment to remind me that "looking through" is sometimes the best approach to complete an impossible mission. In terms of procrastination, "looking through" a task instead of "looking at" it forces you to keep moving, no matter how boring, tough, or inessential the task may seem.

There are no perfect conditions. It might never be the right time to start working on your new business idea. You might just as well start now and see how it goes, adjusting, tweaking, and learning as you move forward. As the writer Oliver Burkeman puts it: "Uncertainty is where things happen. It is where the opportunities—for success, for happiness, for really living—

are waiting."[20] A healthy dose of uncertainty may become your most effective weapon to reduce your procrastination tendencies.

---

[20] Oliver Burkeman, *The Antidote: Happiness for People Who Can't Stand Positive Thinking* (New York: Farrar, Straus and Giroux, 2012).

2.7 Comparing yourself and your business to others

What if the grass is greener on the other side? Would my freelance business prosper if I moved to another country, changed my logo, hired a mentor, rented a better office space...? The list of potential improvements seems to be endless, especially if you can't stop comparing yourself and your business to other freelancers, entrepreneurs, or founders. There was a period in my early freelancing days when I was absolutely convinced that renaming my business and redesigning my logo were the only ways to grow. I had attended countless branding sessions on translation conferences and concluded that to work with bigger (read: better-paying) companies, I needed to rebrand. Obviously, there are many other factors that can help you establish yourself as a serious, professional entrepreneur. A unique logo or well-thought-out business name is just one of many pieces in this puzzle. However, for some reason I couldn't stop thinking about the amazing breakthrough that would await me once I changed my company name and logo. I went down the comparison rabbit hole without checking if all the other fancy names or branding elements really would attract better-paying customers. At that time, the freelance translators' world consisted of creative individuals running their businesses under names such as Rainy London Translations, Want Words, or Point2Point Translations, which made my DP Translation Services— created ad hoc and without any branding expertise—seem remarkably ordinary.

Soon afterwards came another obsession: my business was located in the wrong country. By listening, talking, and interacting with other freelance translators, I realised that the optimal location for your business is where your clients are, which is usually the country of your source or target language. Of course, my location was far from optimal. I was a Polish translator living in the Netherlands, working in English and German. Since my Dutch wasn't at an advanced level, I believed that the only way to make my business prosper was to move to an English or German-speaking country. Moving back to Poland was out of question. Alternatively, I could work on honing my Dutch skills until I'd be able to translate from Dutch as well. Somehow, I failed to recognise that in the age of globalisation, the location of a freelance business doesn't really matter. If I wished to, I could even choose to live in Kuala Lumpur and still attract, serve, and maintain customers looking for quality IT translation into Polish. The endless comparison game moved my focus away from my strengths and shifted it to my potential defects. That's the worst place to be. It's hostile, dark, and not conducive to growth and creative thinking.

I hope you'll never reach that place, but if for some reason you can't stop burying yourself in unhealthy comparisons, here are some ways in which you can put an end to this game.

Compare yourself to yourself

"I wish I could move to another country to pay less taxes like my friend does. I'm sure I would have more clients if I rented a marvellous space like my competitor did. I wish I had started my business earlier like A, B, C did..."

Playing the comparison game is pointless. There are thousands of freelancers and business owners who are doing great, but what you see in the media rarely reflects the reality. Most businesses talk only about their highlights, and most freelancers only display their moments of success. They probably wouldn't publish an article about all their failures and the mistakes they made before they succeeded, and they wouldn't post pictures showing how they lost money, customers, or their reputation. If you compare yourself and your business with others, chances are you'll get stuck in paralysis-analysis. Especially when you compare yourself with people who started earlier than you. They have had more time to learn and more experience making the same mistakes you're probably exposed to now.

If you love comparisons, it's time to move your focus and compare yourself only to your past self. Think back to the moment when you just established your business. Analyse the first two years of your activity. Can you see how far you've come from that point? How much you've progressed? How much you've accomplished? You might be thinking: "Yes, but it could still be better/faster/bigger/more profitable or different in many other ways..." It certainly could. But your business might have also taken a wrong turn or ceased to exist. If the pandemic, inflation, or some other nightmare didn't crush you and you still run your freelance business, earning money by doing what you love, you can consider yourself successful. Other occurrences are just extras that may or may not have happened. Whenever you're tempted to compare yourself with others, look back at yourself five, 10, or 15 years ago. You've made great decisions, developed your skills, crossed paths with amazing people, and survived many crises. Are these reasons not good enough to celebrate? Your past self would probably admire your present self.

Look for inspiration

Every freelancer, founder, or business owner comes from a different background. We all have different ideas and were shaped by different people and environments. If there's someone you look up to, take their business as an inspiration rather than a source of negative comparisons. Find out what they did to overcome their obstacles, how they approached their marketing strategies, or who they collaborated with to achieve their goals. Treat their success story as motivation to experiment and grow your business. What worked for them may or may not work you, but you won't find out until you try.

I have a Moroccan friend who is a brilliant shoemaker. He also spends a great amount of time on his phone taking pictures, videos, and streaming live to share pieces of his world. When he opened his business in a fancy district of Los Angeles, his Instagram account suddenly exploded. With all the famous clients that were visiting his shop and all the videos and photos he took of them, he quickly became a social media star. Other brands perceived him as an influencer and started collaborating with him. His creative content and designs became his second source of income, almost equivalent to what he had been making in his shoe-repair shop. I do admire his persistence, craft, and people skills. But what worked for him wouldn't work for me: Our businesses are different, we are different, and our clients have very different mentalities. I could go down the comparison rabbit hole and decide that I also need to constantly be online, shoot videos, talk and make jokes to grow my business. But that's simply not me. Even if I followed in his footsteps, you would still be able to hear my shaky voice in my videos or sense my fake enthusiasm. I'm better off using his story as a source of motivation. It could be my reminder that it's fine to bring my personality to my business, that people love to connect with people, that whatever I do, I have to keep it real. With this positive comparison, I can take a moment to figure out how and when I can be more private with my customers or how I can add a bit of my personality to my social media posts. If you need to compare yourself with others, do it with a growth mindset, searching for potential tweaks and ideas that you could add to your business.

Own what makes you different

Karl Lagerfeld, the former creative director of Chanel, once said, "Personality begins where comparison ends."[21] That's a perfect summary of why eliminating negative comparisons is so crucial. If you understand who you are, what makes you and your business different, you'll be less likely to feel intimidated by other people's success. To reach this state of mind, you can list everything that sets you apart from others: What is your story, experience, strengths, and zones of genius? How do all these aspects shine through your words and actions? How can your business benefit from your personal uniqueness?

Be proud of who you are and acknowledge your business achievements. You don't have to be among the Forbes 500, be awarded a spot on the 30 Under 30 list, or earn a six-figure income to feel accomplished. You and your business are unique without all these fancy titles. Find out what is it that makes you stand out and highlight it whenever you can: in your marketing materials, when you communicate with your customers, or when you mingle with other freelancers. With this approach, you will realise that you don't have to compare yourself to anybody else. All you need is to focus on your goal to keep

---

[21] As per his official Twitter account: https://twitter.com/KarlLagerfeld

innovating, moving forward, reaching new milestones, and living the (business) life you think is best for you.

Limit triggers

Another way to stop the habit of comparing is to become more aware of how it starts. Whenever you realise that you're comparing yourself to someone else, think back to the moment that triggered this thought. Maybe you saw a post on social media or heard an interview on a business podcast. Maybe you were scrolling though LinkedIn and read about your colleagues' achievements. Identify your triggers and limit your exposure to them. In my case, it has always been social media. Self-proclaimed experts, collectors of university titles, happiness braggers, wealth promoters—these were the people that used to intimidate me. My perception of their success paralysed me to the highest possible degree. Luckily, I acted before it was too late. I banned myself from social media, limiting my interactions only to reading and answering messages. When I wanted to post marketing content on my business profiles, I used an external tool (Hootsuite), so I wouldn't be tempted to check other entrepreneurs' stories. After some time, my trigger was fairly under control, and I learned to take everything I see on social media with a pinch of salt.

Comparing yourself and your business to anyone else is counterproductive. The grass may or may not be greener on the other side, but wherever you go and whoever you become, you'll still be a part of the same human society, where hurdles are an inevitable part of the journey. One of the eight limbs of yoga in Patanjali's Yoga Sutra,[22] called Niyama, refers to the duties we have towards ourselves. It includes one very important approach that can be useful in your fight with endless comparisons: santosha (contentment). This duty implies being satisfied with what you have without comparing yourself to others. In our society that keeps telling us to always strive for more and making us feel unsatisfied with what we have, santosha can be an effective antidote. It reminds us that we can simply take the present moment for what it is and feel complete. Eliminating comparisons or wishful thinking helps us to find true joy. Joy that comes from within. It's worth practising santosha both in your private and business life to make sure that the comings and goings of other people and situations have no impact on your self-esteem or your level of happiness.

---

[22] Patañjali, *The Yoga Sutras of Patanjali. the Book of the Spiritual Man*, trans. Charles Johnston (London: John M. Watkins, 1975).

3. Extra tools to help you fight your obstacles

Now that you know how to identify and cope with the most powerful enemies of your success as a freelancer, it's time to add extra weapons to your arsenal. Even if you overcome your fears, beat your imposter syndrome, quit procrastinating, defeat your perfectionism tendencies, and stop comparing yourself to others, you might still be exposed to unpleasant situations. Depending on your definition of success, you'll need to equip yourself with new skills and habits. A selection or combination of these extra tools will help you stay focused, motivated, assertive, compassionate, and curious in your business. You can use them to overcome the main hurdles discussed in the previous chapter, or implement them as quick fixes whenever you find yourself slowing down on your fearless path towards your goal.

Let's have a closer look at these six tools and find out how they stand to benefit your business life.

3.1 Keep developing your skills

After many years of running your freelance business, you may start thinking that you know it all. There's nothing that will surprise you, there's nothing new to explore, there's nowhere to go to boost your expertise. That's a totally normal assumption. But that's all it really is—an assumption. In fact, it's your ego shouting out loud and holding you back from understanding the real picture. Every industry is constantly changing. It could be moving at a faster or slower pace, but it's still moving forward. As a responsible freelancer, you have to keep up with the recent developments in your field. Whether you're a photographer, developer, marketer, translator, accountant, physiotherapist, or consultant—you need to find resources to keep developing both your professional and business skills. If you fail to do that, you may end up losing your customers, income, and your reputation. The stakes are too high.

It's not enough to become an expert in your field. After all, you run a business, so you need to add business skills to your repertoire as well. Good communication, problem-solving, customer care, marketing, sales, time management, project management, networking...the list is long. No one person can be perfect in all these areas, so you can either delegate some tasks or identify your weak points and work on them to progress to the next level.

Where to start?
Developing your skills doesn't necessarily mean signing up for endless university programmes, masterclasses, or online courses. It could be as simple as visiting conferences, reading

books and magazines, or engaging online with other professionals. With the variety of resources available online, it's easy to get overwhelmed or fall into the "I have to be everywhere" trap. This is a typical problem especially common among fresh graduates and new freelancers. I've experienced it as well. Long before the pandemic paralysed the event industry, I believed that I had to attend every single translation conference in Europe—whether as a regular attendee or as a speaker—or attend every single webinar. This approach was of course time-consuming and not necessarily cost-effective. My fear of missing out was so overwhelming that I kept registering for new events and booking my flights and hotels, not only to sharpen my professional skills, but also, or maybe above all, to meet like-minded people. Yet another excuse to travel. Luckily, I came to my senses in time, as it would have been hard to keep up this pace in the long term. I realised I needed to stop being chaotic with my professional development and start planning better. Instead of booking conference tickets on a whim, I began to draft a budget and schedule my courses and conferences in advance.

Create your plan
Before you go to extremes in any direction—either believing that you know it all already or constantly chasing more development opportunities—draft your plan. For example, once per year, you can write down all the areas relevant to your expertise in which you'd like to improve your skills or knowledge. Then choose optimal resources: a course, book, set of articles, workshop, or any other event. Finally, allocate a yearly budget for your education. It also helps to schedule days or hours during the week that would be fully designated for honing your skills. You can block a time slot in your calendar,

such as every Wednesday morning, or block a couple of days when you'll be studying new resources rather than doing client work. Of course, a perfectly crafted plan will be of no use if you don't stick to it. Make sure to follow your schedule, even in hectic times when acquiring new skills is the last thing you want to do. The truth is, there will never be a right time to read all the books or attend all the events you so desperately want to tick off on your to-do list. There's nothing wrong with rescheduling your growth activities when you get swamped with work, but to make the most of your courses, events, or conferences, you'll need to find a way to prioritise them. This is how you can force yourself to work on your business, not only in your business.

If you can't block out time on your calendar for regular education, try taking a few days off during the year. It's like a holiday, but instead of swapping your office for a beach, mountain hike, or sightseeing, you'll spend a few days on updating your skills. You can inform your customers in advance and explain why you won't be available for a couple of days. Your professional development matters. With your new skills, you'll be able to support your customers in a better way and run your business more effectively. That's a win-win for everyone. To make this time a bit more like a real holiday, you can take your training to another location. Outside or inside, to a rented apartment or a hotel, to a cafe or library.

Once you find the right location to execute your plan and eliminate all distractions, immerse yourself fully in your courses, books, events, or one-on-one consultations. You might be surprised at how much you learn if you focus on studying only. For example, to complete most online courses, you'll need only about two to three hours. If you group several courses into your "professional development holiday," you could complete as many as six courses in three days! It may sound overwhelming, but it's definitely doable.

If taking a few days off for professional development is out of the question, there's one last option: use public holidays to learn and grow. Not all holidays are exciting and packed with family visits. Sometimes a public holiday is peaceful and uneventful. You could use those opportunities to take your skills to the next level, especially if your "to-learn" list keeps expanding. Maybe your family members will be glad that you found yourself an immersive activity, as they might also prefer to spend the day on their work and hobbies. You could still spend a few hours together while working on your separate plans. It may not sound like the best way of celebrating a public holiday together, but sometimes there's nothing special going on (hello, lockdown!) or the weather is uninviting. Why not use such a day to sharpen your skills and get ready for brighter days?

Be fully present

It's easy to get carried away with planning and end up scheduling far too many activities. Try to stay realistic, and above all, ask yourself one important question: How will I make sure I can absorb the new bits of knowledge? How can I put my new skills into practise?

Without an efficient system for capturing new information, you'll quickly forget what you've learned. Your enthusiasm may also wear off when you come back to your routine. To be able to implement all the new tips, ideas, or tools, you'll need to prepare in advance. Decide how to take notes, where to store new information, and how to ensure you remember the main takeaways from your courses and conferences. It can be in a digital or paper form, on Post-it notes or digital notes displayed as your PC background. It could be a video or voice recording that you listen to while driving or cleaning—figure out what works best for you. Finally, eliminate any distractions such as incoming e-mails, phone calls, or social media notifications. If you attend an online event, it's probably not a good idea to multitask during the session, for example, listening to the speaker while working on a project. This is highly ineffective. Believe me, I tried it too many times...

Put your ideas into action
Once your course, conference, or workshop is over, it's time to implement your new skills. Sieve through your notes and analyse the key messages. Maybe it's the detailed explanations about tools that you need for your work. In this case, try them out, experiment with new techniques to make sure you can use the tools to improve your processes. If the course inspired you to make little tweaks to your business, use the momentum and do it right away. If you feel motivated to implement bigger changes, break them down into smaller chunks and schedule your tasks. The key to success is to do as much as possible before your initial enthusiasm evaporates. It also helps to look back on what you've achieved from time to time to make sure you don't slip back into old patterns. Even if you updated your knowledge or changed something in your business right after your training, don't forget to check where you stand as time goes by.

For example, if a course you attended motivated you to start using social media in a more effective way, make sure that your great results will last. Set aside time every month to review whether you are still following your new strategy. Even if you're swamped with work, take a break to assess your progress. If there's anything that isn't going as planned, try to fix it. Otherwise, you'll soon find yourself searching for more courses, more books, or more training sessions on the topic you've tried to delve into so many times before.

Gain a fresh perspective

Running a freelance business means that only you decide what skills should be developed and when. Sadly, it's easy to push a potential development plan to the back burner, or even worse, start to believe that you're too smart, too skilled, or too knowledgeable to follow yet another online course. To gain a fresh perspective on your development, you can try to search for ideas outside of your industry. Pick a new field and peek into the life of other freelancers and business owners. For example, you could follow social media accounts or register for events that have nothing to do with your line of work. If you're a translator, engage with programmers, carpenters, or graphic designers. If you're a mobile app developer, have a look at profiles of people working in the legal or medical industry. Maybe this shift of perspective will help you find new processes, new tools, and new resources that you can implement in your business. Maybe you'll meet someone who will inspire you to change the way you think about your services or marketing strategies.

That's what happened to me when I started connecting with business owners from different fields via Instagram. I suddenly discovered a new world of opportunities. By following one brilliant shoemaker (mentioned in Chapter 2.7), I got inspiration and courage to make my social media content more engaging, and by following some book reviewers' accounts, I came up with ideas on how to promote my book. There are countless sources of inspiration. All you need to do is look beyond your industry with an open mind.

Developing your professional and business skills while working on paid projects is like walking on thin ice. One wrong step, and you can end up immersed in freezing water, trying to stay afloat. To be on the safe side, plan ahead, follow your strategy, and never stop learning.

3.2 Plan your freelance journey

To plan or not to plan—that is the question. There are people who love to meticulously draft their career paths, set goals for their businesses, and visualise their growth and progress. There are also those who prefer to improvise, keep their eyes open for interesting opportunities, and grab new chances as they appear. When you run a freelance business, you won't be able to get away without planning, at least to some extent. You don't have to pin down your every move, schedule the whole year in advance, or know exactly where your business will be in five, 10 and 15 years (although that helps!). The minimum you need to do is to define who your clients are, how much profit your business should generate, what your core processes are, and which educational activities you need to engage in. Building a safety cushion is crucial as well to be able to survive in tough times. Finally, don't forget to rest. If your business doesn't generate income when you don't put in the work personally, think about ways you can save up for your annual holiday and keep your customers engaged while you're away.

Plan ahead, but stay flexible

Even if you plan ahead and know exactly what to do to grow your business, leave some room for unexpected changes. Luckily, as a freelancer, you're the only one who decides what projects to take on, who to collaborate with, or which opportunities to take. Don't limit yourself to your meticulously crafted schedule. Try to stay open to new proposals that might be beneficial to you and your growth. Sometimes the best things in your (business) life will come unplanned. For example, my long-term vision for my business never included me teaching at a university. Of course, the thought of "Oh, it would be great to share my knowledge at a reputable university one day" crossed my mind a few times, but I never did anything to convert that thought into reality. The only thing I did was to create an online course. Two years after I published my website-localisation course for translators, I was contacted by a programme coordinator from the KU Leuven University in Antwerp, Belgium. She asked me if I would be interested to teach a class on website localisation at their university, and I couldn't resist. Accepting this offer meant that I had to tweak my plans and agree to commute from Amsterdam to Antwerp every second Friday to give a four-hour class to a group of translation students. All these efforts were well worth it. My unspoken dream came true. I tried my hand at teaching post-graduate students, learned a lot about myself while preparing and teaching the classes, and ultimately figured out what it is that I really (don't) want to do as a freelance business owner.

When you leave room for flexibility, you can easily adapt to new trends, embrace changes, and adjust your business processes. A huge dose of that adaptability became necessary during the coronavirus pandemic, when many entrepreneurs had to pivot to keep generating income. For example, one law firm from Connecticut[23] noticed that there was a rise in domestic violence cases, so instead of marketing their other services, they focused on offering help in this area only.

---

[23] https://www.dcfdefense.com/

The lockdown also inspired one famous hairstylist to create an online course on how to cut your own hair at home,[24] and many fitness studios started live streaming their classes to students locked in at their homes. There are many ways in which you can adapt to new opportunities and circumstances once you know how to meet your customers' urgent needs. But to be able to recognise those opportunities, you have to keep listening, watching, analysing, and being open-minded.

Think short term and long term

For a very long time, coming up with a five, 10, and 15-year goal for a business was standard procedure. Freelancers adopted this approach as well. However, with new digital technologies, and later with the global pandemic, many entrepreneurs realised that long-term plans can easily fall apart. The world is changing too rapidly, and nearly every industry evolves so fast that it might be difficult to keep up with the pace. "Long term" may not mean 15 years anymore, but merely two or five. Whatever that number is in your case, make sure that you have at least a draft of your long-term vision. A good approach is to first define your big picture (a.k.a., your definition of success), and then break it down into little actionable steps. Your big picture will be your long-term plan, and the details will fill in your short-term agenda. For example, if your goal is to become a bestselling author, you can ask yourself these questions:

What do I need to write a bestselling book? What topic should I address, what should be my writing style, my target audience?

---

[24] *How to Cut Your Own Hair at Home, According to Celebrity Hairstylist Jen Atkin* (Good Morning America, 2021), https://www.goodmorningamerica.com/style/story/celebrity-hairstylist-jen-atkin-demonstrates-cut-hair-home-69938131.

Do I have resources to self-publish it, or do I need to contact a publisher? If so, will I need an agent? How much time would I need to write the book? How much time would the publishing process take? How should the book be promoted to reach the bestseller's list? And which list: New York Times? Amazon? In a general category or in a specific one?

With this approach, you'll be able to assess whether your goal is attainable and define all the ingredients required for your recipe for success. Going backwards from the big picture to specific tasks will help you come up with an action plan and time frame. That's your long-term vision. If there are more accomplishments on your success list, scrutinise each of them, break them down into details, and add them to your timeline. Of course, make room for unexpected circumstances, bearing in mind that you always need capacity to adapt, react to an imminent threat, or grab a once-in-a-lifetime opportunity.

Use visualisation to follow your plan
No matter how precise your plan is or how motivated you are to follow it, sometimes putting your ideas into action will become challenging. Perhaps another freelancer comes up with a similar idea for a unique product you wanted to create. Maybe you figure out that you need help from others to move forward, or perhaps you get stuck due to a lack of resources. There's no magic formula to convert your plans into reality, but one thing is certain: visualisation helps.

As soon as you put your plan on paper (or save it in an app), close your eyes, and imagine it becoming true. Use all your senses: Notice the smell of that book you want to publish, delight in the taste of those artisan muffins you want to sell, feel the surface of those ceramic dishes you want to produce, see the smile on your customer's face, hear the sound of payment notifications as transfers go into your bank account. The more details you can imagine and feel with your senses, the more realistic your goal will appear. This method will also help you figure out what it is that you really want. Maybe your plan is exciting on paper, but once you visualise all the details, you might recognise that it's not the right choice for you. Once you come up with the most suitable plan for your business, don't abandon it when you experience the first obstacle. Look at your plan regularly, find out if there's anything you can do now to be closer to your goal tomorrow, and use the power of imagination to visualise your plan becoming reality.

3.3 Define your goals and priorities

Your plan won't be effective if you don't start by defining your goals and priorities. Only then will you figure out what matters to you the most, what is worth your attention, and where your resources should be invested. With your goals and priorities sorted out, it will become easier to navigate your commitments, responsibilities, and business ideas.

Choose three to free up more space
To reach a healthy balance in your business and private life, you'll need to keep it simple. When you limit your priorities, you'll also limit your choices, potential distractions, and diversions. That's how you can simplify everything. It's like keeping a boat on course—you can't cruise in all directions simultaneously to reach to your destination. It's better to select one specific route at a time and stay on track. Otherwise, your journey might become too long, or you might run out of resources.

To be on the safe side, identify a maximum of three priorities that will guide your life. Of course, your priorities don't have to be set in stone. Review them every year or each time a major event occurs in your life. A balanced priority mix might include your health, your family, and your business. For example, your priority in terms of health could be making healthy choices for yourself every day; in terms of your family, you may want to decide to be present for them whenever they need you; and in terms of your business, you can choose to always put your customers' wishes first.

You could focus on one priority only or choose three priorities for your business alone, ignoring your social life and your health. But that's the quickest way to lose your sanity. For a harmonious and accomplished lifestyle, you need to feel comfortable in three areas: professional, social, and personal. This means being satisfied with the work you do, having enough quality time with your friends or family, and taking care of your well-being. That's why picking one priority from each category is a smart move that will enable you to strive for a good combination of personal, business, and social priorities.

Stay on the right track

If you're not sure what your priorities are, ask yourself what the things are that are so important to you that you couldn't imagine giving them up. Maybe what you tend to consider crucial is relevant only in a given moment. To establish your priorities, you need to think in the long term: What will matter to me the most in the next six to 12 months? Where do I want to direct my full attention? What really inspires me to work harder? When am I willing to agree on trade-offs or sacrifices?

Once you answer these questions, you'll probably end up with a long list of priorities. Picking only three items will seem nearly impossible, especially if you're a polymath. Fear not, for there's a way out of this maze of possibilities. For example, you can assign a value to every priority on a scale from one to 10. If this leaves you with too many 10s, assign a time frame to each item, choosing between a three-, six-, and 12-month period. Your current top priorities are the items that take the least time to attain but have the highest value. The rest can be temporarily pushed down the list.

If concentrating on merely three areas is still too overwhelming, you can promise yourself to update your priorities every year. Working on too many long-term priorities simultaneously is usually very stressful and exhausting.

Once your priorities are pinned down, it's time to define your goals.

Goals vs. priorities

Priorities and goals are different things and shouldn't be confused. A goal is something that you'd like to achieve in the future. It's an area in which you're willing to invest time, effort, and energy. Ideally, your goals should serve your priorities. For example, if your priority is to generate more passive income in your business, your goal could be to create a subscription-based product in the next 10 months. If your priority is to increase your profit, your goal could be to acquire at least three more regular customers in the next six months.

Cut it down

When you're exploring your goals, make sure to stay true to your priorities. Yours—not those of your friends, your colleagues, or society. It's easy to mistake someone else's voice and expectations for your own. Take the time to listen to your inner wisdom and figure out what it is that you want to achieve. Where does your heart lie? Do this both for your business and your private life.

The best approach is to choose one goal per priority. Otherwise, you'll end up working on too many items, which will only delay your progress. This is especially important when you work solo, without delegating or collaborating with a team of specialists. The fewer goals you focus on, the more you'll be able to achieve. It's like multitasking. Carrying out many activities at the same time (for example, driving a car and calling a friend, writing an article and checking social media), won't help you accelerate. Instead, you'll only slow yourself down and waste your resources. When you multitask, you lose time and energy as you constantly switch between different activities. The same applies to your goals. It's hard to work on several different objectives at the same time. You could still reach the finish line, but it might take longer or exhaust you physically, mentally, and emotionally. Multitasking or working on multiple goals can also make you less productive and increase your chances of making mistakes.

Choosing one goal per priority, but with full energy, focus, and creativity is the best approach if you value your mental health. You'll be surprised at how much faster you can progress if you move towards one destination at a time. When you reach it, you can stop for a while, enjoy where you are, and come up with a new target if needed.

The art of alignment
The final step in determining your goals and priorities is to make sure you align them correctly. In this way, you can eliminate distractions and avoid working on someone else's goals. And that's the key to making your definition of success come true.

Once your goals are aligned with your priorities, you'll need to make sure your actions serve them as well. Everything you do, including how you plan your day, how you use your time, and what projects you accept, should help you reach your goals and stay true to your priorities. For example, if your priority is to spend quality time with your family every evening and you receive a business proposal that would significantly limit your chances of achieving that, you could decline the offer to stay true to your values. If your goal is to gain three more regular customers in the next 10 months, you'll probably need to allocate more time to client-acquisition strategies and eliminate conversations or actions that don't serve this goal. But to be able do this, you'll also need to learn how to set boundaries.

3.4 Learn to protect your boundaries

There are moments when I'm extremely proud that I've been running my business for nearly 12 years. Proud and relieved. Especially when I hear stories about the peculiar corporate reality. Recently, one lady shared an experience with me that perfectly demonstrates why responsible introverts are usually on the losing side in the harsh corporate world. She was working hard, complying with all her manager's requests, working overtime, and saying yes to nearly every new project and idea. She was patiently waiting for a token of appreciation. A raise, a compliment, encouraging feedback. But it never happened. After several months of silently hoping for a promotion, she collapsed. Another (male!) employee got promoted while her efforts were totally ignored. My friend, one of the hard-working lady's colleagues, asked her a very straightforward question: "Have you ever asked for a raise? Have you ever told your manager how you feel?" The answer was a dry no. The obedient introvert never protected her boundaries, and she never expressed that she felt undervalued. Motivated by my friend, she finally spoke up and…her wishes were granted. She received what she had silently hoped for: a raise and a promotion. But she could have avoided many disappointments and sleepless nights if she knew how to ask for what she deserved and how to protect her boundaries.

Set boundaries
Learning to protect your boundaries is an extremely important skill, whether you're an employee, freelancer, or serial entrepreneur.

It's easy to get caught up in the daily grind—simply ticking off the tasks on your to-do list, doing without thinking, running without stopping, looking without seeing. It's easy to lose your focus while you get swamped with work. That's why setting boundaries and learning to protect them is a vital survival skill. It's like a compass that will help you keep moving in the right direction.

Once you align your actions with your goals, you'll need to reject anything that doesn't serve them. That means saying no firmly, without any apologies. Before investing your time and energy into any activity, verify that the new task is in service of your goal or is compatible with your priorities. If it isn't, simply decline it. You can refer a new client to someone else or explain that you don't have capacity to work on a new proposal. Practise saying no daily, even to small requests. In this way, you'll get ready for bigger no's in the future. You'll stop wasting your time on things that do not matter at all.

Protect your boundaries
Setting and guarding your boundaries will help you structure your time in the best possible way. When you do only what matters to YOU, you can make the best use of your time and keep working on your definition of success. This is also the best method to save your energy and avoid distractions. For example, one way to stop wasting your invaluable hours is to keep your phone or other mobile devices away from your bedroom. When you use your smartphone as an alarm clock or take your phone to bed, you're creating a temptation that might be too strong to resist. If the first thing you do when you open your eyes in the morning is to look at a mobile screen, you'll probably start checking your e-mails or social media before your mind is ready to be bombarded with news, updates, and

requests. If you use your phone in your bed in the evening, it might be difficult to disconnect and fall asleep. Setting clear rules about how and when you use your phone is an example of guarding your boundaries. You probably don't want to scroll mindlessly through irrelevant content or fall into a comparison rabbit hole after checking photos of your friends on social media. To guard your boundaries, you need to consistently remind yourself of your goals and priorities. You need the courage to speak up when someone wants to cross one of your boundaries. You need patience to let people realise that you take your boundaries seriously, and you have to put yourself first every single day.

Learn to say no

Obviously, it's difficult to protect your boundaries if no one knows about them. Your colleagues, partners, or family members might not be aware of your priorities, so it might be wise to clearly state where the limits are. For example, if a customer asks you for a video conference, you can tell them in advance how much time you can allocate to the call. This will help you stay focused and productive without wasting time on issues that could be discussed at a later point or via e-mail. If a member of the parents' community at your child's school asks you to get involved in an upcoming event by baking cakes and setting up decorations, but such actions clearly don't align with your priorities, simply say no or find an alternative solution that will help you protect your boundaries. Instead, you could support the event by bringing healthy goodies purchased at the local shop.

Saying no or suggesting workarounds might sound overwhelming at first. But it's just another skill you can learn with a bit of practise. Yes, some people will view you as arrogant or selfish. Yes, you won't always be perceived as nice, friendly, or helpful. But that's a good sign. You can't be everything to everyone. The opinion of other people, especially strangers, shouldn't matter to you. Don't be afraid of negative reactions when you say no. If something doesn't align with your priorities, a polite no is the only wise response you can give.

3.5 Find your community

Teamwork, community, hierarchy—that was never my cup of tea. One of the main reasons I wanted to become a freelancer was to avoid working with people. I couldn't have been more wrong. When you sell products or services, you'll ultimately have to deal with people. Even if you never get to see them. It took me years to realise that online communication also counts as working with people. There's no way around it, unless you focus solely on trading stocks, crypto currencies, or options. But even when you don't have to communicate regularly with people to generate your income, you still need others to be able to hone your skills, stay up to date with the news, exchange your thoughts, and share your stories. Humans are a tribal species, designed to evolve together, not to live in silence and seclusion. Many studies confirm that the need for social connection is as important as food and shelter.[25] 250 million years of evolution have predisposed our brains for social interaction. Belonging to a tribe and communicating with others is essential to our survival. In his book *Social: Why Our Brains Are Wired to Connect,* Matthew Lieberman[26] claims that our brains relate being more successful to being more social. The importance of social connection is so strong that if we are rejected by others, our brains interpret it in the same way as when someone hurts us physically. To be innovative, to thrive, to feel happy and appreciated, we can't eliminate people from our life. That's why finding your tribe is so essential.

The power of belonging

As a freelancer you usually work alone, which might be very isolating. There's no one to cheer you on, no one to motivate you to develop your skills, and no one to support you if you need to vent. That's why belonging to a community pays off. It's difficult to keep up to date with several communities (think of all the LinkedIn or Facebook groups that you've joined throughout the years...), so the best approach is to focus on two or three tribes, where at least one is related to your business activities and one has nothing to do with your work. You can find a group of other freelancers who will understand the struggle of finding new clients, managing your time, and being your own boss. Belonging to such a group will also provide you with many networking opportunities and increase your chances of being recommended to your colleagues' clients. Your second tribe could be related to your industry. In this way, you'll be able to stay abreast of recent developments, exchange news and ideas with other people working in your field, or ask for suggestions if you get stuck on a project. Finally, your third tribe could be related to your passion. There's life outside of work as well, even if you are a business owner. Connecting with people with similar hobbies will help you detach from your duties and responsibilities and shift your energy to what you enjoy the most. A good place to find such a community might be at a sport's club, fitness centre, yoga studio, on a course, or at a local church. Nothing replaces regular contact with real humans, so don't limit your communities to online

[25] Stuart Wolpert, "UCLA Neuroscientist's Book Explains Why Social Connection Is as Important as Food and Shelter," UCLA Newsroom (UCLA, October 10, 2013), https://newsroom.ucla.edu/releases/we-are-hard-wired-to-be-social-248746.

[26] Matthew D. Lieberman, *Social: Why Our Brains Are Wired to Connect* (New York: Crown, 2013).

groups only. Being able to read body language, see gestures, keep eye contact, and get a handshake or a hug is extremely crucial for your mental health. No online interaction can replace that.

Belonging to a community that respects you, supports you, and listens to you will help you create the "whose factor" mentioned earlier in Chapter 2.2. When you know you belong somewhere, you gain more confidence to enter new territories. You always have a friendly place to come back to, no matter what happens. That's extremely important, especially if you struggle with your self-worth or are hounded by unfounded fears.

Finding the harmony

This all sounds great, but what if you really don't have time to socialise? If that's the first thought that comes to your mind when you hear the word "community", it's time for a slight change of perspective. The truth is, you're the only person who decides how much you can contribute to your tribe. For some people, it will be enough to meet in real life once per month and chat online from time to time. Some will want to contribute daily, by organising events or starting online discussions. Find what works best for you, but don't disappear for long periods of time, neglecting your community. Give it as much time and energy as you can, knowing that you can always increase or decrease your presence as your amount of work fluctuates.

Belonging to a community might also become addictive, especially if all communication takes place online. Make sure you set rules for yourself and protect your boundaries. Starting every day with two hours of online interaction in various groups will probably limit your productivity and drain you of energy that could be better spent working on your clients' projects. The challenge begins if social interactions are your main source of motivation. Some of my freelancing friends consider working in isolation to be a sort of punishment, so they constantly switch between working on their projects and chatting online. If you also suffer when you need to spend long hours in an empty office, a compassionate community could be a powerful antidote. But still, you will have to make sure that your workday doesn't include socialising only. There are also people like me—introverted and reluctant to engage in excessive social contact—who will only join a community if it's absolutely necessary. Both approaches, or anything in between, are perfectly fine, as long as you can maintain the right balance between work and active participation in your tribe. Whatever happens, make sure your communities serve you, don't belittle you, make you feel depressed, or demotivated. Evaluate regularly whether your dearest community hasn't become poisonous. You can ask your family or friends for feedback, or simply listen to their cues. For example, my husband once accused me of bringing home bad energy every morning. At that time, the only thing I did every morning was to drive to a yoga studio, practise ashtanga yoga, and then drive back home. It was up to me to figure out whether it was the time spent in traffic or the atmosphere in the studio that made me feel low. Once I identified what the problem could be, I had no choice but to change some parts of my morning routine.

There are many places where you can find like-minded people, grow together, exchange ideas, and have a regular dose of human interaction. From professional associations to industry platforms, local clubs, cafes, libraries, or fitness centres—you have the freedom to choose your tribe and benefit from social connections on every single level. Both in your business and your private life.

3.6 Give back to your community

Once you find your supportive tribe, don't forget to support others as well. It's easy to remain passive, asking for help without helping, taking without giving. No matter how far you are on your freelancing journey, there's always something you can share with other freelancers, business owners, and community members. You don't have to limit your support to the professional area only. More importantly, you don't need to treat your community in a transactional way—helping only where you are supported, sharing your knowledge only with the members that supported you. The beauty of all human relations begins when you act selflessly—giving without any expectations, sharing without waiting for a reward.

You've probably seen hundreds of social media posts with "handy tips" or blogs with "tips and tricks." While this is a perfect strategy to showcase your expertise and to attract fans or potential customers, don't expect the nuggets of wisdom you share online to help your profits skyrocket. It's not about increasing your sales (although freebies can help to boost your income). It's about a simple human need to give back. To uplift others. To share your experience. To help others avoid potential traps.

How can you do this?

Mentoring
One method to give back to your community is to volunteer as a mentor. There are many professional organisations that offer mentoring programmes to their members. Both the mentee and the mentor can benefit from such a relationship: learn, grow,

and get motivated to explore new areas. When I first volunteered as a mentor for Professional Women Network in Amsterdam, I didn't expect it to be such an eye-opening experience. By supporting other female business owners, I realised what my weak and strong points are. Our relationship forced me to reconsider my business activities. Ultimately, as a mentor I learned much more than as a mentee. By giving without expecting anything in return, I suddenly noticed a wide ocean of opportunities. Maybe you can embark on a similar journey as well, to thrive by helping others to grow?

Teaching
Online or face-to-face, at conferences, networking events, schools or universities—you can share your knowledge in a formal or informal way. You could do a short presentation for the members of your professional association or participate in a growth programme for students from your alma mater to motivate them and tell them about career opportunities. You can also run a podcast for other freelances or record online videos to show professionals in your field how to solve some common issues, how to use specific tools, or test new methods of work. There's always something you can share with others, not necessarily for money. Even if you think you're not an expert, there's always someone less experienced than you. Maybe your tips will be life changing for those who are just starting their careers?

Giving presentations and teaching at a university was definitely life changing for me. Although my goal was to help and inspire others, I grew my skills and knowledge every time I had to speak in front of my audience. It was a transformation on all levels: leaving my comfort zone, overcoming my fears, and honing my skills to help others expand their knowledge. It's a truly addictive experience if you enjoy trying new things and changing the definition of what you think is (im)possible.

E-books

You can also transfer your wisdom into an e-book to share it for free with other freelancers, students, or professionals in your field. Writing is a self-exploratory process in which you constantly redefine your ideas, gather your thoughts, and acknowledge your valuable experience. By helping others figure out how to navigate their life or career, you'll also gain more clarity around your own values. But here's the question that might be lurking at the back of your mind: Haven't all possible topics been covered already? Yes and no! Perhaps everything you would like to share with others has been discussed many times before, but there's one thing no one mentioned yet: your own experience. Maybe there are hundreds of e-books about vegan recipes or social media marketing, but none of them includes your perspective, your life lessons, your anecdotes. Instead of copying popular textbooks or mixing and matching quotes, give your story a personal touch. Don't be afraid to experiment with style, content, or layout, but also don't force yourself to be innovative if you're not. Free e-books are usually short, so you can share your knowledge on a very narrow topic. For example, if you're a photographer, you can share five tips on how to create the most effective light for shooting portraits outdoors. If you're a nutritionist, you can explain what vitamins and minerals are the best to fight fatigue. If you're a developer, you can share your ideas on how to write cleaner and better code. There are many specific subjects you can delve into, as long as you make sure your e-book helps to solve a particular problem, is relevant to your community, and reflects your own experience.

E-mails and conversations

Once you become an established freelancer you might realise that there's one more interesting perk that comes with it: you're asked for advice in the least expected situations. E-mails with CVs from strangers aspiring to be your interns or co-workers, messages on social media with requests for support, small talk at networking events filled with "Can I pick your mind?" questions. These are perfect opportunities to give back and share your invaluable experience. While it's impossible to reply to all unsolicited e-mails or engage deeply in a conversation when you only have two minutes to spare, you can still make a difference in someone else's life. If someone sends you a terrible resume hoping to work with you, you can quickly explain that you're not looking for new employees and indicate resources on how to create a more professional resume. If someone approaches you on LinkedIn asking for advice on how to tap into your field, you could share several links to valuable courses, websites, or books. It will cost only a few minutes of your time, but for the person seeking help, those few minutes could pave their way to a better life. Of course, if you receive hundreds of requests for advice every day, you probably won't be able to reply to all of them. But you can still save someone else's world by finding at least five minutes per week to answer a few people waiting for your valued feedback.

The perks of giving back

It's easy to get stuck in a transactional mindset and share your advice only when you receive something in return. Money, credit, material rewards of any type. The problem with this approach is that it prevents you from experiencing something far more valuable: human connection, expressions of pure gratitude, the smile on your mentee's face, the aha! moment in the eyes of a student who timidly asked you for a tip. In fact, giving back to your community has numerous advantages that can be obtained only when you act out of a pure need to help others. As Tony Robbins puts it,[27] the secret to living is giving. Real meaning doesn't come from material possessions or from the things you get, but from everything you give. Supporting others doesn't only benefit your community. It uplifts you. Research has shown that if you volunteer, your level of happiness increases, and at the same time, your likelihood of suffering from depression decreases.[28] Your physical health benefits as well: It has been proven that giving back to your community can lower risk of hypertension.[29] What's more, by supporting others, you can turn away from your own problems, gain a fresh perspective, and develop new skills. Volunteering is also a great way to expand your network and discover new ideas or opportunities. Who knows, maybe by helping that stranger in your sports club you'll stumble across a new potential client? Maybe someone will be so inspired by your advice that they will mention you to their friends, and so your reputation will grow.

---

[27] Anthony Robbins, *MONEY Master the Game: 7 Simple Steps to Financial Freedom* (New York: Simon & Schuster Paperbacks, 2016).

[28] Peggy A. Thoits and Lyndi N. Hewitt, "Volunteer Work and Well-Being," *Journal of Health and Social Behavior* 42, no. 2 (2001): p. 115, https://doi.org/10.2307/3090173.

[29] Rodlescia S. Sneed and Sheldon Cohen, "A Prospective Study of Volunteerism and Hypertension Risk in Older Adults.," *Psychology and Aging* 28, no. 2 (2013): pp. 578-586, https://doi.org/10.1037/a0032718.

Supporting your community—whether it's related to your work, hobbies, or society in general—fulfills your deepest human needs. When you contribute without expecting anything in return, you feel needed. You feel unique. You're one step closer to becoming selfless. That's how you give back what you've received, preserving your valuable skills for the next generation.

4. Other things to remember

Is there any guarantee that once you overcome your fears, eliminate negative thought patterns, avoid limiting behaviour, and surround yourself with a supportive community, you'll be soaked in success? I don't think so. There might be a couple of more stumbling blocks in your way. Whether or not you measure your success by the amount of money you earn, it helps to assess your approach to finances and material possessions. Money is not all that matters in a freelance lifestyle or work in general. Without authentic connections, passion, and the ability to act on time to adjust to changing circumstances, your freelance adventure probably won't be fulfilling. After all, why would you care about having more, act faster, or be better if you can't share all these benefits with your loved ones? What's the point of reinventing and minimising your work schedule if you can't use the "extra time" for doing what you truly enjoy?

In the last chapter of this book, I'd like to share five ingredients that will help you enrich your recipe for a satisfying freelancer's life: your approach to money, work, and time, willingness to adapt, and empathy.

4.1 It's not only business that matters

If you're surrounded by representatives of Generation Z or Generation Y (more commonly known as "Millennials", and yes, I belong here as well), you must have heard of Garry Vaynerchuk (more commonly known as Gary Vee, and yes, I used to be his dedicated fan as well). In his multiple books and online videos, he stresses that only constant hustle will help you achieve your dreams. While I love his content-related tips and admire how quickly he responds to new trends—from opening one of the first e-commerce stores in the 1900s, to tapping into social media before it became a big hype, to launching an NFT collection in 2022 right before the market crashed—I'm sceptical about the hustle culture he so aggressively promotes.

Essentially, hustle culture preaches that the harder you work, the bigger the reward. But what happened to working smart? What's the point in working non-stop, sleeping two hours per day, and focusing on business only? Why would hustling make me happier? Can it really make me richer?

The sad truth is that hustling is not a universally realistic scenario. Investing significant time, money, and energy into your project to convert it into a serious start-up to eventually grow into a huge company seems to be a privilege reserved for the lucky few. What works in the U.S. may not work in Europe, Asia, or Africa. The reason for this is simple: There are different tax systems, social benefits, cultural values, and business ethics in every single region. The revered "from zero to hero" or "from rags to riches" attitude sweeps the painful side effects of hustling under the rug. And painful they are: One study found[30] that people who work 55 hours or more per week suffer from increased blood pressure, heart problems, and have a greater risk of developing depression or succumbing to unhealthy habits such as smoking, which further deteriorates their health. Hustling negatively impacts our psychological health as well: One study[31] confirms that working more than 50 hours per week decreases productivity and ultimately leads to burnout. Even Gary Vee, the King of Hustlers, admitted that his passion for work made him neglect his health,[32] so he hired a full-time employee who would focus on managing his health only.

What's the point of all that hustle? Why would you give up so much and live only for your business ideas? Is constant hard work the only way to achieve success?

The Unhustle Culture
There's a remarkable beauty in silence. In slowing down. In being rather than doing. While there's nothing wrong with following your passion, pursuing your goals, being ambitious, or working hard on your business, you shouldn't let your business life overpower you. The main problem with hustle culture is not the detrimental impact it has on your mental health. It's how contagious it is.

---

[30] Ashley Chen and Sherilyn Wen, "Psychological and Physiological Effects of Hustle Culture," ed. Stephanie Sahadeo, Race to a Cure, January 25, 2021, https://www.racetoacure.org/post/psychological-and-physiological-effects-of-hustle-culture.

[31] John H. Pencavel, "The Productivity of Working Hours," *IZA Discussion Paper No. 8129*, April 26, 2014, pp. 2052-2076, https://doi.org/10.2139/ssrn.2429648.

[32] *Taking Your Health Seriously As A Hardcore Entrepreneur | A Gary Vaynerchuk Original, YouTube* (YouTube, 2017), https://www.youtube.com/watch?v=e9U8aVVW34c&ab_channel=GaryVee.

Parents who buy into the idea of hustling may easily transfer this attitude to their children, bringing up the next generation of chasers, hustlers, non-stop doers. In many regions, children are pushed to attend extracurricular classes and after-school activities. Ballet on Monday, swimming lessons on Tuesday, modern dance on Wednesday, theatre on Thursday, and judo on Friday. Oh, and the chess club and gym class sounds so nice as well, not to mention extra language classes—kids as young as four years old are already being introduced to hustle culture. This is how they learn that having free time is unhealthy. They grow up convinced that any unplanned day is a day that's going to be wasted. What happened to fun and creativity? The best ideas—whether you're a child or an adult—come to us in moments of silence. In the sweet act of "not doing anything," you can find answers to the most burning questions—whether it's finding out that dolls can't fly or why no one wants to buy your product.

Another problem with hustle culture is that you might easily get lost in the hustle. You may lose your "why". Are you driving yourself into the ground to make more money? To possess more stuff? To grow your business to an enormous size? Or maybe the constant busyness is just an excuse. It's a good reason to ignore your fears, addictions, or worries. Grinding is a good distraction to thinking. That's how it was for me. For a very long time, my business used to be my priority. I would spend more than 50 hours per week working both in and on my business. It became my addiction, which pushed other—more serious addictions and anxieties—to the background. I forgot about my passions: yoga, swimming, reading, or learning. The only thing that mattered was attracting more customers, growing my account, delivering more projects. Until I realised that my workaholism was just an extension of eating disorders that I suffered from as a teenager. Uncured anorexia and bulimia slapped me in the face as an adult because the core reasons behind them—anxiety and the feeling of not being enough—were still there. Rather than addressing the main culprits and embracing the fact that I am enough, I kept hustling to achieve a vague, material confirmation of my "enoughness". Of course, it only made matters worse.

Hustle culture is toxic. You can easily lose your balance and forget about life outside of work. Hustling may quickly merge into workaholism that provides you with a constant flow of dopamine, like any other addiction. The more you add to your schedule, the more indispensable you feel. The more your colleagues, clients, and partners appreciate your work, the more addicted you get to their attention. You finally find external validation of your personality and skills. You feel valued and you keep going. In most cases, the tendency to constantly focus on work comes from feeling empty inside. Hustling is an easy way to forget about your traumas, health problems, anxiety, or loneliness. It's a perfect substitute to spirituality. If you suspect you are caught in the claws of busyness and your business has become your priority, force yourself to stop for a minute and ask yourself a very simple but powerful question: Why? What are you really trying to achieve? What are you trying to hide?

Don't get me wrong. I'm not condemning hustlers, hard workers, or grinders. Everyone has their reasons for putting in extra hours of work. Everyone has a different definition of success. The key is to not lose your perspective. Your business is just a (small) part of your life. There are many other ingredients to a fulfilled and successful life: health, family, friends, passions, spirituality. No matter what you're trying to achieve, remember your "why" and make sure that your health always stays at the top of your priority list. Higher than your business, and higher than any possessions.

4.2 It's not only money that matters

Chasing money is just another addiction. It's a vicious cycle, because the more you have, the more you want. The more material possessions you accumulate, the more you need to invest to protect them. Think about car or household insurance. About all these extra cameras you believe you need to install in your garden to protect your house from trespassers. The extra maintenance costs for your multiple vehicles, wardrobe, or equipment. When your business keeps blooming, it's easy to fall into a materialistic mindset. If earning multiple digits per month is on your list of goals, it's helpful to build a healthy approach to money. In other words, it's wise to practise non-attachment.

In "The Yoga Sutras" of Patanjali,[33] non-attachment plays a key role in a mindful, peaceful life. It doesn't only apply to yogis. Practising non-attachment is beneficial for people from all walks of life. We all tend to be attached to something: to our families, our belongings, or work. This concept is often misconstrued as indifference or total rejection of the materialistic world—that would be a hard mission to accomplish, especially if you have a business to run and a family to feed. Rather than withdrawing from the physical world, non-attachment suggests focusing on the world as it is, not on how we think it should be. It implies putting effort into whatever you do, but without being fixated on the outcome. In this way, you'll learn to see everything from the right perspective: as passing clouds that come and go. It's not the result that matters. It's not the amount of money you earn, it's not the ambitious goal you have to achieve, it's not the difficult skill you can master. Being obsessed with your results will only lead to disappointment, especially if things don't go as you had imagined. With non-attachment, you can see the world as it is. You can concentrate on the act of doing—whether it's promoting your business, pitching to new customers, decorating your house, practising yoga, or learning how to drive. That focus on here and now, without the fixation on the outcome, will help you enjoy the process and become mindful of sensations that are caused by your "doing". Why would you care about those sensations? Because that's how you become more aware. That's how you can learn more about yourself and the surrounding world. When you're aware of your feelings, emotions, or physical reactions caused by a specific action, you'll also learn how not to react to them. If you're not aware of these emotions and reactions, your mind becomes prone to "impurities" that may overpower you. These could be thoughts, judgements, events, situations, people, or habits. One such habit is fixating on money, a common cause of suffering.

But isn't this a contradiction? After all, in the business world one needs to be focused on goals and revenue, so why would non-attachment help you?

Let's have a look at some examples of how practising non-attachment can benefit your freelance business life.

---

[33] Patañjali, *The Yoga Sutras of Patanjali. the Book of the Spiritual Man*, trans. Charles Johnston (London: John M. Watkins, 1975).

Fixation on goals and money

In the pursuit of my goal, I could easily get attached to the idea that my freelance business will only prosper if it generates 10,000 euro per month. Convinced that this is my highest priority, I'd draft detailed plans, schedule marketing campaigns to attract more customers, prepare another promotion to upsell more products to my current clients, and create free online courses to increase my passive income. I'd put in all the hard work, come up with creative ideas, and even collaborate with promoters who'd spread the word about my courses and amazing services. However, what if, as the end of the month approaches, I realise that I'm 2k short of my goal. Desperate to achieve my magical 10k, I'd publish more promotional posts and send more private messages on Twitter, get super active on LinkedIn, and follow up with all potential clients who are still in the "let me think about it" stage. The result? My social media contacts unfollow me, discouraged by my aggressive marketing, my Twitter account gets temporarily suspended due to overactivity, and my potential clients don't reply to my follow-up e-mails because they need more time to consider whether they want to buy another course that they might not even be able to complete. Instead of reaching my goal, my fixation on the outcome led me to making the wrong decisions, which could now decrease my chances of generating my magical amount next month. How would non-attachment help me here to find a better way to serve my clients, my business, and myself?

To start with, I should probably verify whether my goal is realistic. Do I really need a five-figure revenue? What if my business generates only nine thousand? Isn't that a good enough reason to celebrate? What about eight or seven? Next comes the intention behind my actions. I should check whether the focus of all my marketing campaigns, social media posts, and newsletters is on selling or showing potential clients the benefits of my products. It's not about me. It's about them noticing what's in it for them once they buy my course, book, or consulting session. Then come my actions. Can I be indifferent to rejections or lack of reactions to my content? Am I sure that a strategy I assumed isn't for me wouldn't work better? For example, if I'm attached to the idea that recording YouTube videos is not my cup of tea, perhaps I should reconsider that? Maybe I could record short educational videos and subtly hint that more tips are included in my courses, rather than just focusing on writing promotional materials. Can I get rid of thought patterns that obviously don't lead to any results, or am I so attached to my ideas that I keep repeating the same strategies, hoping that someone will finally notice how brilliant my product is? Finally, once I realise that I'm still too far away from reaching my goal, maybe instead of pushing and repeating the same actions, it's wiser to take a step back, get to know my target audience better, tweak my marketing to their preferences, or add more income streams to my business.

Non-attachment is all about eliminating your preferences, your mental models, prejudices, and reflexive reactions to events, people, and situations. It's not about giving up, withdrawing, or becoming less ambitious, but rather about being more aware. It implies making sure your emotions, memories, or likes and dislikes can't impact how you interpret the world around you.

Enjoying the process

In many cases, non-attachment to results will help you achieve better results. How is that possible? When you focus on the task at hand and try to perform it as well as you can, chances are you'll end up with a decent outcome. However, when you're only thinking about how rich, famous, or successful you'll become after publishing your mobile app/book/online course/website, you might easily get distracted. In this state of mind, you're more likely to rush through your projects, make bad decisions, or take shortcuts. This has happened to me many times whenever I lost my perspective: from hasty trading decisions, to collaborating with people who promised unreasonable miracles, to using unsuitable tools that were supposed to make my work faster. Attached to my goals and deadlines related to profit, I ignored so many other important things and ultimately, instead of converting my ideas into a "passive-income machine," I ended up back where I started, perhaps with even less income. On the other hand, whenever my focus was not on making X amount of money in Y amount of time, but on giving my best to the project, guess what happened? Yes! The results were better than I had expected. Because I didn't expect anything. I was merely very enthusiastic about the process itself, whether it was creating presentations, writing articles, or recording online courses. Passion attracts attention. Sooner or later, the products you create with enthusiasm will find recognition and appeal to more people than those ideas implemented purely for money.

The right perspective

Practising non-attachment to results might be easy when things are going well. But it gets more complicated when everything seems to fall apart. When you lose your clients, receive disappointing feedback, your taxes are higher than you expected, or when a digital product you worked on for many long months doesn't resonate with your customers. Faced with so many negative results, keeping a positive mindset might be a mission impossible. The good news is, you are the only one who determines your attitude. A positive approach is a choice, not something that emerges once you succeed. After many years of research, Dr. William Glasser introduced his revolutionary Choice Theory,[34] implying that the only person whose behaviour you can control is your own. What you receive from other people are only bits of information, and it's up to you to decide how you interpret or react to them. By choosing a specific behaviour, you're showing your reaction to the stimuli you have received from the outside world. But the most important part is that you and you alone can control your reactions. You can choose whether you want to become furious when a client rejects your offer or stay calm, take a few breaths, and analyse what might have gone wrong with your proposal to draw conclusions for the future. With some effort, you can also influence the way you think and feel. How does this relate to non-attachment? Well, since you can control your behaviour, thoughts, and emotions, you can make a conscious decision to stay balanced even on rocky ground. To persevere in this commitment, you can practise gratitude: Start your day by listing the five things you appreciate the most in your life. Then,

[34] William Glasser, *Choice Theory: A New Psychology of Personal Freedom* (New York: HarperCollins Publishers Inc, 2011).

every evening, think about five pleasant situations from your day. This exercise will help you put everything into perspective and shift the disappointing results to the background. However, the core of both non-attachment and consciously choosing your behaviour is a solid foundation. It's easy to get obsessed with your business when it becomes your priority. And in most cases, it becomes your priority because you forget what matters in your life. Healthy you, healthy family, healthy environment—this is the strong base that you'll need to prioritise. When you take care of your body and soul, when you make sure your family stays happy and healthy, you build a safety cushion. It will always be there to help you land safely, no matter what turbulence you go through in your business life. With this solid foundation, practising non-attachment to money and business results becomes more enjoyable.

4.3 Sometimes you need to give up to speed up

Freelancing is not all roses. Sometimes you may hit a wall and start questioning your goals, actions, and ideas. Am I still going in the right direction? Maybe after 100 rejections it's time to give up? But how do I know that number 101 won't be successful? You don't. In most cases, the decision whether you should give up comes from your intuition. Statistics, cold-hearted calculations, and long talks with your friends or mentors can be helpful as well, but ultimately, the right answer lies within you.

As Marc Randolph puts it in his excellent book *That Will Never Work: The Birth of Netflix and the Amazing Life of An Idea*,[35] sometimes giving up is not giving up per se. For example, at some point Randolph, the co-founder and first CEO of Netflix, decided to leave the company he created. However, he didn't consider this move as giving up—quite the contrary. The company Netflix had become throughout the years wasn't the same company he initially envisioned. He recognised that it was time to go his own way for him to be able to evolve and stay true to his passion, which is to build start-ups rather than run huge companies.

Giving up to free up

There are many different reasons you may decide to give up on your business idea or the whole freelancing career. It could be due to lack of money, lack of time, or lack of patience to wait until your brilliant ideas convert into profitable reality.

Very often, we lose something much more valuable: our passion. If your business activity, products, services, idea, or career doesn't intrigue you anymore, it might be the right moment to implement changes. It's time to choose another direction. Without passion, you won't be able to improvise and adjust on the go to figure out how to make your plan work.

Giving up on your projects, ideas, or collaborations will sometimes help you create space for more valuable opportunities. It might be painful to leave the project you have invested so much time and money in, and it might be even more difficult to leave a business you helped to create. About six years ago, I had what I thought was a brilliant idea: organising real-life workshops for translators in the Netherlands. I teamed up with a colleague who had all the skills I lacked to make sure this project would become reality. She was the talker, I was the doer. We put a lot of effort into designing the brand of our All-round Translator project, spent countless hours on social media marketing, invited brilliant speakers to decent venues, organised regular half-day workshops and a yearly one-day mini conference, each time in a different city in the Netherlands. We didn't do it for profit, but rather to share our passion for educating, meeting new people, and upgrading our skills at the same time. Until one day when my passion died. After nearly three years, my role as a co-founder, co-manager and co-organiser of these events became a dull duty rather than an exciting venture. Our project didn't generate any profit, but it didn't matter. We were breaking even, which was a good enough result. Eventually, I decided to leave the project to my

---

[35] Marc Randolph, *That Will Never Work: The Birth of Netflix and the Amazing Life of an Idea* (New York: Little, Brown and Company, 2019).

colleague, who was still passionate about our initial idea. Leaving my "baby" wasn't an easy decision, but I had to make room for a real one: I was about to become a mother. That's why my priorities started to shift. In hindsight, I consider quitting my role at the All-round Translator a reasonable step. By giving up on tasks that were neither exciting nor profitable, I created more space for the work I really loved. Plus, I avoided the harsh reality of navigating real-life events during the pandemic and lockdowns that arrived soon afterwards. It seems my intuition guided me well.

Give up to find yourself

What would you call a person who puts tremendous effort into converting their concept into reality, works long hours to create a unique product, designs beautiful social media profiles to attract more attention, invests in materials and tools to ensure perfect results, finally sees the concept come to life, only to step away from the project after its successful launch? Is he a quitter? Is she a loser? Are they out of their minds?

As a persistent and committed person, I could never understand how anyone could simply abandon a project without waiting until it generates at least a fraction of the expected results. But after 10 years of living with someone who I'd have earlier called "a loser", I realised that it's not about giving up. It's about having a passion for building. There's a reason most start-ups have both a founder and a co-founder. You can't possibly have all the skills and knowledge to build a successful business from scratch. Some people are builders, some are maintainers. Some people love to manage people, others prefer to research, calculate, and plan. There's nothing wrong with leaving "your" project behind after the long building phase.

This simply means that you're the builder and you need someone else to manage the project and make it profitable.

This is what happened to me. My husband is an ideas person. He can come up with thousands of ideas for what seems to be an original business or side hustle. He would even spend several months on creating, designing, researching, and building a product or service, and then...walk away from it. He repeated this pattern of building and then abandoning great concepts for many years. I saw countless ideas come to life and then crash and disappear before reaching their maturity. It was painful to witness such great potential going to waste every single time. Finally, I stepped in and suggested that I be the "maintainer" of his ideas that have merely seen the daylight. That's how I ended up being a manager of a women-focused NFT project. As the more patient and persistent one of our duo, I could spend hours on PR, marketing, growing our social accounts, and maintaining our community, while the builder next to me could start a new building process without any regrets.

In the book *The Unfair Advantage*,[36] Ash Ali and Hasan Kubba explain what it takes to succeed in the business world. As they say, "It's not enough to be in the right place at the right time; you also have to be in the right state of mind." It's not hard work or luck that determines your success, it's listening, being observant, and acting on an opportunity when it shows up. But that's not all. Although we might already have what it takes to convert our dream into reality, without the right traction, that amazing idea will never find its home in the material world.

---

[36] Ash Ali and Hasan Kubba, *The Unfair Advantage: How You Already Have What It Takes to Succeed* (New York: St. Martin's Press, 2020).

And that's when it's time to recognise that your only choice is to give up—whether you want to switch from full-time employment to freelancing, or from freelancing to serial entrepreneurship. However, that step of "giving up" is an essential part of the growth process. Sometimes it's wiser to abandon your project, team, or idea so that you can find yourself and answer the questions: What is it that I really want? What is my passion? Can I convert it into a (freelancing) career?

Give up to slow down

Sometimes giving up will help you free up space, time, and energy for what matters the most. Your priorities will probably change as you get older, or maybe you'll notice that there are different cycles in your life: a few years of prioritising your family, followed by a few years of focusing mainly on your business, only to realise that what really matters is your health. Every "focus cycle" comes with its own distractions that won't serve you until you give something up. You can't be everywhere and do everything, both for your business, your family, and yourself. Trying to run too many projects at the same time will limit your brainpower, exhaust your energy, and steal your sleep. For example, if your goal is to attract more customers, don't run several different campaigns simultaneously. If you feel a constant flow of inspiration for many ways of bringing in more clients to your ecosystem, write everything down and analyse which is the best place to start. Free e-book? Free online courses? Speaking at conferences? It all may sound effective, but unless you're a super(wo)man, you probably won't be able to create all these things at the same time. Spreading yourself too thin by working on several strategies at once will slow you down. Alternatively, you can delegate some tasks so that your ideas can come to life without you losing too much of your time, your patience, and your true self. As surprising as it might be, focusing on your priorities will help you find the space to fit everything else in, although not necessarily at the same time or to the same extent.

4.4 Don't sell your time, sell your skills

When reaching your goals seems like a long journey, you might be tempted to put in more. More work, more hours, more energy. According to a survey conducted by Freelancer Map,[37] a platform for freelancers from across the world, the majority of freelancers work between 31 and 50 hours per week. At the same time, most full-time employees in the European Union work 37 hours per week,[38] while in the U.S., this figure lies at 38 hours.[39] Longer hours don't necessarily mean higher income, even though many freelancers report generating a higher salary compared to their previous full-time jobs.[40] But why should we, the courageous freelancers who chose independence instead of comfy perks and a regular salary, replicate the typical work pattern of full-timers? Didn't we become freelancers to be free? To escape the rat race and the standard 38- or 37-hour work week?

What if we put more "free" back into "freelancing"? It's time to gain more freedom and ditch the constant exchange of time for money. No matter what your definition of success is, you should act wisely. Instead of working hard, work smart. Make sure you get paid for your skills, not only for your time. How can you do that? One way is to generate passive-income streams.

Create once, benefit forever

Passive income means more security. If you suddenly lose your customers, need to take a longer holiday, your health deteriorates, or if you need to limit your working time due to family commitments—a passive stream of income will allow you to cover your expenses even if you can't actively work. Especially the last few years—marked by the pandemic, followed by inflation and the global polycrisis—proved that our economic situation may unexpectedly be turned upside-down. Even the most profitable businesses might be forced to close their doors, and the most successful freelancers may suffer a sudden revenue drop. With passive income, you'll be able to weather the storm and adapt smoothly to inevitable changes. How can you add a passive-income stream to your freelance business?

Online courses
No matter what industry you work in, you can always convert your knowledge and experience into a steady source of passive income. For example, you can create an online course based on your area of expertise. If you're a freelance photographer, you could teach others how to take portrait or wedding pictures. If you're a graphic designer, you could teach others how to use a certain tool or where to find inspiration for amazing designs. If you're a developer, you could create a course about building

---

[37] Viktor Marinov, "How Many Hours Do Freelancers Work? [Survey Results]," Freelancer Map, December 7, 2020,
https://www.freelancermap.com/blog/freelancer-hours-survey/.

[38] "Working Hours by Country and Industry," Clockify, September 1, 2017,
https://clockify.me/working-
hours#:~:text=On%20average%2C%20a%20full%2Dtime%20employee%20in%20the%20European%20Union,(40.4%20hours%20per%20week).

[39] Alison Doyle, "What Is the Average Number of Work Hours per Week?," The Balance (The Balance, September 7, 2022),
https://www.thebalancemoney.com/what-is-the-average-hours-per-week-worked-in-the-us-2060631.

[40] Upwork, "Freelancers Union and Upwork Release New Study Revealing Insights into the Almost 54 Million People Freelancing in America,"
Upwork.com, n.d., https://www.upwork.com/press/releases/freelancers-union-and-upwork-release-new-study-revealing-insights-into-the-almost-54-million-people-freelancing-in-america.

mobile apps in Python or Java. The possibilities are endless. All you need to do is define your target audience, find a specific problem that your course will solve, and structure the content into easily digestible modules. Of course, you'll need some sort of recording equipment and video editing skills, but the good news is you don't have to spend fortune on professional gear. You could shoot your online course with only a good-quality smartphone. To learn how to edit your content, you can either watch a few short online tutorials or...hire a knowledgeable freelancer who could do it for you.

Although online courses require some initial work, once you publish your content, you will only need to update it from time to time and find the right marketing strategy. You can schedule posts on your social media to promote your course and make sure you get featured in other media (for example, via the HARO platform) to talk about your course. You could also find affiliate partners with large audiences who could promote your course for a commission. For example, for my online course "How to translate and localize websites: Level 2," I scheduled the promo content for a month in advance, automated my marketing campaign as much as possible, collaborated with four affiliate partners who talked about my course in their social media in exchange for 30% commission, and landed a few interviews via HARO to briefly mention my new products. In this way, once the course was published, I could sit back, relax, and watch my student numbers (and revenue) grow.

Other digital products

Another way to generate a passive source of income is to create digital products such as graphic templates, website templates, e-books, printable colouring pages, calendars, mobile apps, nutrition plans, newsletter templates, and so much more! The key is to use your skills to create something of value that could appeal to a large audience without producing a new product for every single customer. Downloadable templates are a perfect vehicle to achieve this purpose. If you're not convinced, browse Etsy for "CV templates", "printable calendar", or "editable school planner," and let your jaw drop. Some of these items have more than 2000 downloads and sell for as low as 10 euro. You don't need advance math skills to realise that a professionally designed template (plus some marketing tricks) could potentially generate a considerable income. The product you choose as your passive-income stream should be aligned with your expertise, and if possible, linked to your other products or services. Don't just copy what others in your industry do, but convert your knowledge, skills, and ideas into a unique product that will be useful to your target customers.

As with online courses, you'll also need to invest time to promote your downloadable items. Plus, many digital products have a low price point (for example, stock photos or graphic templates), so you'll either have to attract a huge number of customers or add multiple items to your offering to generate decent income. No matter how great your product is, you probably won't hit the magic 1000 or 2000 downloads right after publishing it. Everything needs time to grow. So, instead of constantly checking how many sales your digital product has already made, equip yourself with patience. Keep promoting, expanding, and tweaking your digital portfolio until it becomes your regular income stream.

Blogging

If you don't want to spend too much time or invest a lot of energy in creating courses and digital products, there's one more thing you can do to establish a passive-income stream: sell space on your blog. There are companies out there craving to collaborate with bloggers to promote their products. What's more, they're ready to pay for sponsored articles or offer other incentives. If your blog or social media profile attracts a wide audience, you could turn it into a money-making tool by featuring sponsored items. Just make sure anything you promote is relevant to your audience. Remember that your followers trust you and rely on your recommendations, so remain transparent and support only products that you believe are valuable or can benefit your fans in some way. Your regular readers might get discouraged if they suddenly see a spike in sponsored content. Keep the right balance between paid and regular articles, and figure out what promotion style is the most suitable for your users. Otherwise, your audience might turn away from you and search for another source of reliable content.

Affiliate marketing

If you want to generate passive income with even less effort, affiliate marketing might be the right choice for you. All you need to do is to (skilfully) share products or services created by other companies. The easiest way to start with affiliate marketing is to visit the website of the tools or products you use regularly and search for their affiliate program. Once you sign up for the programme, you'll receive an affiliate link that will allow the merchant to track the people who clicked on the link. When they buy a product through your link, you'll get a commission, usually ranging from 3 to 5%. If you're successful, your commission can build into a decent figure. Like with blogging, you'll need to make sure that the products you recommend really serve your audience and ensure you promote the content in a graceful way. You can share your affiliate links on your social media profiles, on your website, or in your newsletters. Of course, first you'll need to build the right audience who will find the products useful.

Taking it to the next level
To take your passive income to the next level, consider investing in stocks, options, cryptocurrencies, or properties. These investments require significant capital and expertise, so it's wise to consult specialists or talk to people who already earn their income from trading assets. Your income may fluctuate with the ups and downs of the economy. That's why you should probably keep an eye on your open positions and be ready to act before it's too late (a.k.a., before you lose it all). Renting properties can be a great way to ensure a regular flow of money into your account, although the initial investment is usually much higher than in the case of stocks. You can either rent your house in a regular market or on platforms such as Airbnb. Both options have pros and cons, so do your research and decide what works better for you, your location, and your market.

There are many different ways to ensure your freelance business generates income, even without having to spend 30+ hours at work every week. One of my friends used to say that she doesn't believe in passive income, as everything needs either a decent investment or enormous effort to build and market. This might be true, but only partially. Having a passive-income stream doesn't mean that you won't have to work at all. You'll still need to give your energy and attention to your project, but instead of several hours per day as in the case of "active income", it might only be several hours per week. If you're lucky and skilful enough, you might end up with a passive-income project that "runs itself" and requires no or little attention from you. So, before you begin your adventure with passive income, research all available options, decide what method of investing or what type of digital product is the most suitable for you, and take the first steps to create more stability in your business. That's how your "freelancing" will become more "free".

4.5 Don't forget about empathy

When I started attending university at the age of 19, like many other teenagers, I had no idea what my professional future should look like. But, unlike many other teenagers, I became so obsessed with the "where shall I work" concept that I booked a session with a psychologist specialised in female empowerment. She was excellent. But she was wrong about one thing. After analysing my skills, passions, and behaviour, she stated that I'm a creative type who doesn't like pressure. Well, no surprises there. However, she also claimed that I lack leadership skills, self-confidence, and entrepreneurial spirit. In other words, she was convinced that there was no way I would ever become a successful business owner. I felt undermined, to say the least. Having observed my mother who worked as an independent contractor, I too dreamed of being my own boss. Hierarchy, teamwork, artificially imposed responsibilities— none of it appealed to me. Maybe I wasn't good material for a serial entrepreneur leading a multimillion company, but I had what it takes to become a freelance business owner.

In the same month when I wrote my graduation exam at the renowned University of Vienna, I registered my business with the Chamber in Commerce in the Netherlands. My main motivation in becoming a freelancer was to work on my own terms: no boss, no colleagues, no hierarchy. I was never able to thrive in a team. Working solo was like a balm to my soul. But there was one thing I overlooked. No matter what you choose as your freelance business activity, you can't hide from people. There's always someone you need to deal with: your clients, collaborators, accountants, fans, followers, readers, viewers, students... The more services you decide to offer, the longer the list. In my attempt to escape working with people, I found myself surrounded by crowds, even though most of them were only present in the digital world. Then came a lightbulb moment: it was time to tweak my social skills. My psychologist was right: I may have lacked the essential leadership and people skills required to become a business owner. But after several years of running my freelance business against her advice, I learned that nearly any gap in this area can be solved with one important component called empathy.

A secret magic power
Many studies have shown that empathy is not an inborn trait.[41] It's a skill that can be taught. What's more, researchers have found that empathy is one of the key skills in the business environment.[42] With the ability to share another person's experiences and emotions, you can become a more effective leader, a more productive team member, or a better account manager. In other words, empathy helps you communicate. It's an important skill that can affect whether your business will survive.

Empathy helps you to listen better. When you practise empathy in your work, you're more receptive to your clients' needs.

---

[41] Helen Riess, "The Science of Empathy." *J Patient Exp.* 4, no. 2 (2013): pp. 74-77.

[42] Patricia Ann Castelli and Wan Afezah Wan Abdul Rahman, "The Impact of Empathy on Leadership Effectiveness among Business Leaders in the United States and Malaysia," *International Journal of Business, Economics and Management* 2, no. 3 (January 2013): pp. 83-97, https://www.researchgate.net/publication/283721655_The_impact_of_empathy_on_leadership_effectiveness_among_business_leaders_in_the_United_States_and_Malaysia.

You're capable of seeing situations from their perspective, feel their pain points, and understand their problems. With this mindset, your conversations and negotiations become more personal. By showing your clients or business partners that you can see the world from their standpoint, you create better, more memorable impressions. Being empathetic also results in smooth interactions and avoids disappointments. Your clients might not be ready to pay your high rates right now, but if you show them that you do understand that entering into a new business relationship during a recession might not be the best move and wish them endurance in the hard times, they might come back to you when things start looking up again. By listening empathetically, you avoid assumptions and judgements that can hinder communication and destroy relationships. Finally, empathy will help you inspire others: your clients, collaborators, or colleagues. Research conducted by Catalyst[43] shows that having an empathetic leader creates a more inclusive and innovative workplace, which in turn boosts engagement and increases productivity. How does this relate to the freelancer life? Even if you don't manage big teams and have no employees to lead, there are moments in your business life when empathetic leadership skills matter. Take working with other freelancers or collaborating with your accountant, for example. There comes a time when an important decision has to be made, when it's time to roll up your sleeves and get down to work, or when you have to support people around you. This is leadership. Occasionally, every freelancer collaborates with others and takes on the role of a leader. If you lead with empathy, you can create an atmosphere where everyone thrives

---

[43] Tara Van Bommel, "The Power of Empathy in Times of Crisis and Beyond (Report)," Catalyst, 2021, https://www.catalyst.org/reports/empathy-work-strategy-crisis/.

and adores cooperating with you. So, how can you be more empathic in your relationships with your clients and colleagues?

Learning the ropes

The best way to practise empathy is to listen. Truly listen. With patience, without judgement, without thinking what you will say in response. This is the first step towards seeing the world from the point of view of another person. When your colleague tells you she can't finish that important graphic you need for you social media campaign on time because of a serious family emergency, you can try imagining a time when you went through something similar. Maybe you also delivered a project late when your child was sick or when your partner was rushed to hospital. Put yourself in her shoes, recognise what she's going through, and acknowledge her feelings without offering any judgement or solutions. It might be tough to be supportive when your colleague disappoints you, but we are all humans. Shouting at her won't be beneficial to anyone, and it definitely won't help you to progress with your project. Agree on a new deadline and move on.

The easiest way to learn empathy is by talking to people. Be that person in the room who shows interest in others: start the small talk, ask questions. From there, the conversation will flow smoothly and you'll be able to find out more about your potential client, service provider, or colleague. All business relationships—no matter the size of your business—start with people. As a freelancer, you also need to interact with people, as no work is created in a vacuum. Empathy will be your super power, no matter how often you collaborate and communicate with others.

My last two cents

I used to say (and believe) that freelancing is not for the faint of heart. I was not wrong. When you take the plunge into the freelancing world, chances are you lack all the tools required to convert your ideas into a profitable business. But you learn by doing. You keep adding new tools, new connections, new superpowers, and secret weapons until you find your definition of success and figure out how to get there. It took me years to get rid of serious internal and external obstacles that prevented me from achieving my business goals. Not to mention the long journey I had to take to realise what success really means for me. I hope your journey will be shorter and that this book will help you build a freelancing career that you truly enjoy.

Good luck!

References

Ali, Ash, and Hasan Kubba. *The Unfair Advantage: How You Already Have What It Takes to Succeed.* New York: St. Martin's Press, 2020.

Burkeman, Oliver. *The Antidote: Happiness for People Who Can't Stand Positive Thinking.* New York: Farrar, Straus and Giroux, 2012.

Castelli, Patricia Ann, and Wan Afezah Wan Abdul Rahman. "The Impact of Empathy on Leadership Effectiveness among Business Leaders in the United States and Malaysia." *International Journal of Business, Economics and Management* 2, no. 3 (January 2013): 83–97.
https://www.researchgate.net/publication/283721655_The_impact_of_empathy_on_leadership_effectiveness_among_business_leaders_in_the_United_States_and_Malaysia.

Chen, Ashley, and Sherilyn Wen. "Psychological and Physiological Effects of Hustle Culture." Edited by Stephanie Sahadeo. Race to a Cure, January 25, 2021.
https://www.racetoacure.org/post/psychological-and-physiological-effects-of-hustle-culture.

Claire, Marie. "16 Celebrity Quotes on Suffering with Impostor Syndrome." Marie Claire UK, November 10, 2016.
https://www.marieclaire.co.uk/entertainment/celebrity-quotes-on-impostor-syndrome-434739.

Clance, Pauline Rose. *The Impostor Phenomenon: When Success Makes You Feel like a Fake.* Atlanta: Peachtree Publishers, 1985.

Doyle, Alison. "What Is the Average Number of Work Hours per Week?" The Balance. The Balance, September 7, 2022.
https://www.thebalancemoney.com/what-is-the-average-hours-per-week-worked-in-the-us-2060631.

Dweck, Carol S. *Mindset: The New Psychology of Success.* New York: Random House, 2006.

Forleo, Marie. "This Netflix Co-Founder Turned His Idea Into A Company Worth Over $100 Billion | Marc Randolph." Marieforleo.com, June 7, 2022. https://www.marieforleo.com/blog/marc-randolph-netflix.

Glasser, William. *Choice Theory: A New Psychology of Personal Freedom*. New York: HarperCollins Publishers Inc, 2011.

Goulston, Mark, and Philip Goldberg. *Get out of Your Own Way: Overcoming Self-Defeating Behavior*. New York: TarcherPerigee, 1996.

Gray, Krista. "4 Successful People Share How They Triumphed over Imposter Syndrome, the Belief That You'll Be Exposed as a 'Fraud'." Business Insider. Business Insider, January 15, 2019. https://www.businessinsider.com/how-to-overcome-imposter-syndrome-2019-1.

Harvey, Joan C., and Cynthia Katz. *If I'm so Successful, Why Do I Feel like a Fake?: The Imposter Phenomenon*. New York: St Martins Pr, 1985.

Jeffers, Susan. *Feel the Fear and Do It Anyway*. London: Vermilion, 2007.

Jones, Ajayi Luvvie. *Professional Troublemaker: The Fear Fighter Manual*. New York: Viking, 2021.

Kanten, Pelin, and Murat Yesıltas. "The Effects of Positive and Negative Perfectionism on Work Engagement, Psychological Well-Being and Emotional Exhaustion." *Procedia Economics and Finance* 23 (2015): 1367–75. https://doi.org/10.1016/s2212-5671(15)00522-5.

Lieberman, Matthew D. *Social: Why Our Brains Are Wired to Connect*. New York: Crown, 2013.

Mackenzie, Ellen. "How Imposter Syndrome Is Robbing You." *Dishing Up Digital with Ellen Mackenzie*. Episode 4. July 25, 2021.

https://www.ellenmackenzie.com/podcasts/dishing-up-digital-with-ellen-mackenzie/episodes/2147558501.

Marinov, Viktor. "How Many Hours Do Freelancers Work? [Survey Results]." Freelancer Map, December 7, 2020. https://www.freelancermap.com/blog/freelancer-hours-survey/.

Obama, Michelle. *Becoming*. New York: Crown, 2018.

Patañjali. *The Yoga Sutras of Patanjali. the Book of the Spiritual Man*. Translated by Charles Johnston. London: John M. Watkins, 1975.

Pencavel, John H. "The Productivity of Working Hours." *IZA Discussion Paper No. 8129*, April 26, 2014, 2052–76. https://doi.org/10.2139/ssrn.2429648.

Randolph, Marc. *That Will Never Work: The Birth of Netflix and the Amazing Life of an Idea*. New York: Little, Brown and Company, 2019.

Richardson, Alan. "Mental Practice: A Review and Discussion Part I." *Research Quarterly. American Association for Health, Physical Education and Recreation* 38, no. 1 (1967): 95–107. https://doi.org/10.1080/10671188.1967.10614808.

Richardson, Alan. "Mental Practice: A Review and Discussion Part II." *Research Quarterly. American Association for Health, Physical Education and Recreation* 38, no. 2 (1967): 263–73. https://doi.org/10.1080/10671188.1967.10613388.

Riess, Helen. The Science of Empathy." *J Patient Exp*. 4, no. 2 (2013): 74-77.

Robbins, Anthony. *MONEY Master the Game: 7 Simple Steps to Financial Freedom*. New York: Simon & Schuster Paperbacks, 2016.

Sakulku, Jaruwan. "The Impostor Phenomenon". *The Journal of Behavioral Science* 6, no.1 (2011): 75-97. https://doi.org/10.14456/ijbs.2011.6.

Sandberg, Sheryl, and Akiko Murai. *Lean In: Women, Work, and the Will to Lead*. New York: Alfred A. Knopf, 2013.

Savitsky, K., Epley, N., & Gilovich, T. "Do others judge us as harshly as we think? Overestimating the impact of our failures, shortcomings, and mishaps." *Journal of Personality and Social Psychology* 81, no 1 (2001): 44-56.

Simone, Arian. *The Fearless Money Mindset: Broke Doesn't Scare Me*. USA: Arian Simone Enterprises, 2020.

Sinek, Simon. *Find Your Why: A Practical Guide for Discovering Purpose for You and Your Team*. New York: Penguin, 2017.

Sinek, Simon. *Start with Why: How Great Leaders Inspire Everyone to Take Action*. New York: Penguin, 2011.

Sneed, Rodlescia S., and Sheldon Cohen. "A Prospective Study of Volunteerism and Hypertension Risk in Older Adults." *Psychology and Aging* 28, no. 2 (2013): 578–86. https://doi.org/10.1037/a0032718.

Swider, Brian, Dana Harari, Amy P. Breidenthal, and Laurens Bujold Steed. "The Pros and Cons of Perfectionism, According to Research." Harvard Business Review, December 27, 2018. https://hbr.org/2018/12/the-pros-and-cons-of-perfectionism-according-to-research.

Szymanski, Jeff. *The Perfectionist's Handbook: Take Risks, Invite Criticism, and Make the Most of Your Mistakes*. New Jersey: Harvard Health Publications, 2011.

Thoits, Peggy A., and Lyndi N. Hewitt. "Volunteer Work and Well-Being." *Journal of Health and Social Behavior* 42, no. 2 (2001): 115. https://doi.org/10.2307/3090173.

Upwork. "Freelancers Union and Upwork Release New Study Revealing Insights into the Almost 54 Million People Freelancing in America." Upwork.com, n.d. https://www.upwork.com/press/releases/freelancers-union-and-upwork-release-new-study-revealing-insights-into-the-almost-54-million-people-freelancing-in-america.

Van Bommel, Tara. "The Power of Empathy in Times of Crisis and Beyond (Report)." Catalyst, 2021. https://www.catalyst.org/reports/empathy-work-strategy-crisis/.

Vaynerchuk, Gary. *Taking Your Health Seriously As A Hardcore Entrepreneur | A Gary Vaynerchuk Original. YouTube.* YouTube, 2017. https://www.youtube.com/watch?v=e9U8aVVW34c&ab_channel=GaryVee.

Williams, Albert. "What Makes a Critic Tick?" Chicago Reader, July 4, 2002. https://chicagoreader.com/news-politics/what-makes-a-critic-tick/.

Wolpert, Stuart. "UCLA Neuroscientist's Book Explains Why Social Connection Is as Important as Food and Shelter." UCLA Newsroom. UCLA, October 10, 2013. https://newsroom.ucla.edu/releases/we-are-hard-wired-to-be-social-248746.

"Working Hours by Country and Industry." Clockify, September 1, 2017. https://clockify.me/working-hours#:~:text=On%20average%2C%20a%20full%2Dtime%20employee%20in%20the%20European%20Union,(40.4%20hours%20per%20week).

Yates, Jacqueline Laurean. *How to Cut Your Own Hair at Home, According to Celebrity Hairstylist Jen Atkin.* Good Morning America, 2021. https://www.goodmorningamerica.com/style/story/celebrity-hairstylist-jen-atkin-demonstrates-cut-hair-home-69938131.

Found a typo?

While a lot of effort went into ensuring that this book is flawless, it is inevitable that a mistake or two will slip through the net.

If you find any errors in this book, please let me know by visiting:
dorotapawlak.eu/typos

About the author

Dorota Pawlak is a translator, localisation specialist, and a business consultant for freelancers. She is the owner of DP Translation Services and Polish Localisation. She holds an MA in Translation and MSc in Multilingual Computing and Localisation. In 2020, Dorota published her first book, *You've got this: how to continue your freelancing career when you become a mother*, based on the experiences of 15 women from around the world, and her own.

Dorota regularly writes for her blog, where she shares tips for freelancers and small business owners and teaches online courses at www.DorotaPawlak.eu.

Acknowledgements

Special thanks to all the amazing people that I met in my freelancing career: clients, colleagues, mentors, collaborators. Without you, this book would have never happened!

Thanks to my husband, Yassine, who helped me create space and time to write.

Thanks to Julia, my meticulous beta reader, and Susan, my diligent reviewer, who pointed out some inconsistencies and helped to smooth out the rough edges.

Thanks to my mother who instilled the business mindset in me.

One last thing

If you bought this book online and found value in it, I would appreciate if you could take a few seconds to rate it FIVE STARS and recommend it to your friends. If they are also business owners, they will be grateful for your recommendation.

Without stars and reviews, you probably wouldn't have found this book. Please take a moment to support an independent author by leaving a rating.

Thank you so much!

Dorota Pawlak

Printed by Amazon Italia Logistica S.r.l.
Torrazza Piemonte (TO), Italy

41934051R00090